**Shawnee Books**

Also available in this series . . .

Edgar Allen Imhoff

Always of Home

a southern Illinois childhood

Foreword by Robert J. Hastings

Southern Illinois University Press
Carbondale and Edwardsville

95   94   93   4   3   2

Library of Congress Cataloging-in-Publication Data

Imhoff, Edgar A.
   Always of home: a southern Illinois childhood / Edgar Allen
Imhoff; foreword by Robert J. Hastings.
      p. cm.
   1. Imhoff, Edgar A.—Childhood and youth. 2. Murphysboro
Region (Ill.)—Social life and customs. 3. Murphysboro Region
(Ill.)—Biography. I. Title.
F549.M98I45   1993
977.3'994—dc20
   [B]   92-5693
                                                                      CIP

ISBN 0-8093-1853-9
ISBN 0-8093-1854-7 (pbk.)

The paper used in this publication meets the minimum
requirements of American National Standard for Information
Sciences—Permanence of Paper for Printed Library Materials,
ANSI Z39.48-1984. ∞

To my wife, *Betty,*
who has been my best friend
through this book and many other adventures

Contents

CONTENTS

Foreword

Murphysboro, Illinois. Population 8,866—give or take a few. On Route 13, about eighty miles southeast of St. Louis. The setting for Edgar Imhoff's memoirs of his Great Depression boyhood.

As a boy growing up in Marion, twenty-five miles east of Murphysboro, my early memories include hair-raising stories about the great tornado of March 18, 1925, that leapfrogged across Missouri, Illinois, and Indiana, resulting in 689 deaths. When neighbors talked about Murphysboro being "blown off the map," the very mention of the town sent shivers down my back.

Marion had no public swimming pool in the 1930s, and my parents forbade me to swim in "those deep mine holes" north of town, described to me as "bottomless pits filled with brackish, foul-smelling water." But two nearby towns did boast swimming pools, including the one at Riverside Park in Murphysboro.

One time and only one time did I swim in the gleaming, flood-lighted pool in Murphysboro. I think it was the summer of 1940. I went with James O. Dunger, a high school classmate, whose dad drove us in his car. For those kids today who enjoy the luxury of going swimming dozens of times each summer, it is impossible to describe the utter ecstasy of just one night in the Murphysboro pool.

Better still, when we got out of the pool that night, we walked over to the bandshell to hear a patriotic program. It may have been July 4. Anyway, someone stepped out on the stage and, under brilliant spotlights that cast shadows on the big trees nearby, sang "God Bless America."

I'd never heard it before, and I still thrill at the memory.

Although I didn't know him, a ten-year-old boy by the name of Edgar Imhoff was living north of Murphysboro on the "Nolte Place" near the old Number 5 School. Did

Edgar share those magic moments under the starlight on July 4, 1940? I don't know, and doubt if he remembers. But there is one thing Edgar and I have in common—both of us were growing up in southern Illinois during the Great Depression, the biggest economic debacle in American history.

At their lowest point, Edgar's poverty-stricken parents lived in a do-it-yourself, one-room shack with a lean-to kitchen.

In this book, Edgar Imhoff reaches back into his storehouse of memories and shares the warm stories of those years: one-room schools, country churches, family dinners, and doting grandparents.

You're in for a treat as you turn these pages, while Imhoff reminisces about the simplicity of country living, the fun of creating your own entertainment, the dark struggles with poverty and illness, rabid dogs and neighborhood bullies, medicine shows and childhood sweethearts.

Yet it's a beautiful, at times a humorous, story. It rekindles your faith in the magic of dreams and hard work and family togetherness.

Most of all, it's an honest book. The author dares to peel back his emotions and share them with the reader.

This is a rare gift, for most of us hesitate to reopen memories long sealed in silence, fearful they will hurt too much or cause us to long in vain for days that will never come again.

Imhoff kindles the emotion of the reader at the same time he reveals his own emotions. He does this by opening each chapter with an "adult" experience that triggered his memory of a childhood event. Whereas anyone who thinks deeply about life can do this, very few get around to verbalizing those tender moments.

The short chapters make for easy reading. If you're like me, you'll read the book at one sitting. Then you'll go back to relish the moment of the stories that mean the most to you.

And in so doing, you, too, may relive a magic night

when you splashed in a sparkling pool of liquid diamonds, then stretched on the grass to hear, for the first time, "God Bless America."

If so, Edgar Imhoff has succeeded as an author, for good writers not only tell *their* stories, they help readers create and relive their own stories as well.

Robert J. Hastings

Always of Home

Prologue

Taking Inventory

Personal statements about the meanings of our lives are not the common fare of conversations. Sometimes you hear the real stuff late at night in lounges; or, tell someone you'll never see again (night flights across the country are good for that); or, lean over a deathbed to catch a whisper.

And it turns out that what we tell about our lives—when we are really taking inventory—has little to do with what we own or how we make our daily bread. Rather, we talk about who has touched our lives, of how we lived when we thought it would last forever, and always of home. Always of where we came from . . . almost as if we were beseeching the impossible, trying to return there, perhaps to have another chance to start—or not start—down the roads that led away.

What causes one person to leave home while another one stays? Perhaps my own itch to roam came from living by a railroad track during the Great Depression. My mom fed bums who often told of their wanderings as they ate the fare of our little farm. After listening to those whiskered men with their faraway looks, my hoeing of the hard clay soils of southern Illinois seemed awfully tedious. "I'm headin' out west agin' . . . maybe to New Mexico, this time." Their words would echo and echo in my mind. But until I was a teenager, I went no farther than thirty miles from home.

I still have a lot of relatives in southern Illinois. They live in those little towns strung out along the

base of the Shawnee Hills, towns the pioneers settled in order to dig shallow coal from strata bent
upward by the hills.

My relatives know who I am; ask them.
"Why . . . Edgar Imhoff? Let's see. Oh, yeah! That
boy was raised out in the country—about five miles
west of Murphysboro, by old Mt. Joy Church (torn
down now—a shame!). The Ernie Imhoffs lived in a
shack in the woods before they moved to the Nolte
Place, just north of town. Edgar's been gone from
here a long time, but, he was always a good boy—a
smart boy, as I remember."

These are my memories of a home place and a
home people, and of that time when—I suppose—I
was that good boy. The memories were recorded
originally in the form of key words and phrases
entered on the assortment of writing materials one
finds in airplanes, motels, and restaurants. I never
intended to share these memories; then, my daughter, Kat, and my son, Scott, wanted to know about
their roots . . . and Doreen, a dying person whom I
served as a hospice volunteer, enjoyed and encour-
aged my stories . . . and my wife, Betty, a
supporter of all my attempts at creativity, said, "It
would be nice if you shared some of those stories
with Rose and with your folks." And that is how the
scrawl on napkins and ticket folders became these
stories and poems.

The memories are introduced by a sketch of the
circumstances occurring in the present time to
cause me to remember the particular people, feelings, or events narrated. The memories are
presented in chronological order, advancing from
childhood to youth. In addition, the memories are
preceded by and intermingled with typographically
distinct introductory sketches and writings, repre-
senting later times.

2

This book is factual and historically accurate, except that a few names have been changed to protect the feelings of any descendants or survivors. You never know how tender some feelings are going to be—even after all these years.

The Shack on the Hill

The Imhoffs at the shack on the hill, near Mt. Joy
Lutheran Church, 1936.

After testifying to an appropriations commit-
tee, we catch a cab and leave Capitol Hill. My
young associates are celebrating our success in
getting more money for the Program. I decline to
join in; they will discover soon enough that this
town is as much about losing as about winning.

The view down the Mall is as spectacular as
ever. This part of Washington always reminds me
of a mountain valley: massive stone buildings
towering like cliffs above the reflecting pools and
the green stretch of the Mall.

In heavy traffic we are passing the man-made
hill from which the Washington Monument pro-
trudes. People are flying kites of many colors and
shapes. One little boy, in a bright blue jacket, is
having trouble with a long, red dragon kite. It
keeps spiraling downward so that he has to run to
keep it aloft. I can see that he is yelling at his kite,
yelling and laughing. Before we move away with
the traffic, I start to roll down the car window, to
try to catch his words. Then I realize how foolish
that would be—with the city noises—at this dis-
tance.

The Shack on the Hill
(Summer 1934)

The men finished unloading the timbers and
planks from the wagon and stood there in the clearing of the woods discussing how to raise a cabin.
One man tested a foundation stone by trying to
shove it with his foot.

"Ernie, I don't know about these creek rocks. I'd a lot rather see you make some concrete."

"Ray, if I could afford cement, I wouldn't be tearing down an old barn and buildin' a house way out here. It took me a day to set them rocks; they'll last as long as I need 'em."

The three children running between the foundation rocks and in and out of the tree shadows shared none of the labor nor the concern. They played that the big yellow rocks had been put there by Indians and that you could still see the footprints of Indian boys and girls and that the Indians would come back someday.

As the building rose, the men saw that it would never be much more than a shack; there was enough usable wood for one fair-sized room and a lean-to kitchen—that was all. As if to compensate for this disappointment, they concentrated on making the building snug and safe.

"I'd sure like to haul in a load of straw and stuff it in that north wall. Bein' on a hill like this, the wind could freeze you out in the winter."

The children heard none of these words. They were down in the woods looking for the flying squirrel that the eldest child had seen yesterday, as she went to the creek to get water. When the shadow had crossed her path, she had glanced up to see what kind of big bird was swooping through the woods. But, when it landed on a tree, it turned out to be a squirrel! Surprised, she dropped the water bucket. The squirrel, surprised too, leaped from the tree and again became birdlike, gliding through the woods with its arms and legs stretched wide to form a sail.

As the men fitted the tar paper roof around the stovepipe chimney, Ernie kept looking up at a tall tree that stood within falling distance of the building.

"You 'spose we ought to cut down that big white oak? If lightnin' hits it . . . !"

"Wal . . . I would if it was my place."

"Trouble is, I don't own the land—let alone the timber."

Of who owned and who worried, the children cared not at all. Beyond the tall tree—which they had decided covered Indian treasures—the children had found a field of corn so stunted from the hill soil that most stalks held only a single ear. The silk of the forming corn was in full bloom and hung down on the ear not unlike the way hair falls down a human head. That is how the children saw the corn: as blond, red-headed, and dark-haired children; and they gave them human names until they ran out of proper words. But, by then they had more corn friends than they could tend to and they headed back toward the sound of the men hammering on the roof.

Leaving the cornfield, the smallest child stopped by a bent little stalk at the end of a row.

"Goodbye, Mickey. I'll come back to see you. We live here now."

Doreen is dying a little more each day. But her blue eyes are still bright, and she smiles when she talks of her childhood in Arizona and of her Oklahoma heritage. "I like being an Okie," she says. We tell her that last night when we hospice people were caroling outside her bedroom window, we could

look in and see her dressed in a white robe, looking like an angel. She laughs, "Wal . . . I tell you. I forgot all about my pain . . . seein' you all out there with your beautiful faces shining in the candle lights. Edgar, you remind me of my brother. Now, tell me that Christmas story."

The Christmas Fox

It had been a poor summer for Dad. A bad fall followed, and then a worse winter. There were simply no jobs to be had: no work on the hardroad, no hired-man jobs on farms, no work at the shoe factory. Years later, Dad recalled that business activity decayed in the fall of 1934 like the frostbitten grasshoppers and the brown leaves lining the creek beds. He said that it looked like everyone and everything was just going to give up and die.

December came to our shack on the woody hill and found us ill-prepared to survive, let alone be festive. Christmas approached and Dad seemed to become silent and touchy. Two days before Christmas, in a particularly blue mood, he pulled on his boots and wandered a half-mile or so through the woods, for no special reason, to the coal mine Uncle Ray and he had opened by drifting into the side of a hill. They had hauled in a few pieces of battered farm machinery to use in hoisting and moving coal, which now sat idle in the snow.

As Dad walked around the mine portal, stamping to keep his feet warm, he caught a glimpse of something foreign snared in the hoist. It looked like a big fur collar of a coat. He came closer and realized it must be a dead fox—a big and rare silver one, at that. (Years later, when an old man, he told me that at first he could hardly bring himself to touch it.) He held his breath as his eyes ran over the splendid

10

pelt, the leg snared in a wire loop, the black frosty eyes staring at him.

The first we knew of it, Dad showed up at the shack, whistling and carrying a stiff dead animal. He thawed the fox by the wood stove and began to skin it out. We kids made a game out of running around holding our noses and complaining about the smell.

That very day he tacked the pelt on a board, tucked it under his coat sleeve, kissed Mom good-bye, and hiked off to town.

A few hours later, Dad returned from his twelve-mile trip—he had caught a ride home. He came into the shack and put a big sack on the floor. Grinning and laughing he began to pull out oranges, cans of pork and beans, graham crackers, and peanut butter. Then came presents.

Agnes got a Shirley Temple doll, and Charley must've gotten something he liked, but I wasn't paying attention because here came mine: a beautifully painted tin trolley car station, in which two windup cars ran around a little circuit. All night long I kept waking up in the dark shack and reaching out to feel it placed right beside our bed.

Dad never saw another silver fox, and I'll bet no one ever again traded that remarkable a pelt in Murphysboro. And after that winter, things began to get better.

———————————

Leaving home in the morning—a work morning, when you know they are going to beat hell out of you today—is always in hushed tones: lifting the kettle before the whistle; whispering to the cat; closing doors softly; holding home a while longer.

The First Day of School

The first day of school! I could hardly eat my mush and drink the milk Grandma Imhoff had brought down to the shack that morning. It seemed like I had been waiting forever. First, my sister, Agnes, had gotten new shoes and a new dress and gone off to school. Then, my brother, Charley, had put on new overalls and gone to school. Now it was my turn to go away during the day and bring home stories and books.

Today, Agnes was nice about having to tie my shoes and Charley buttoned my new overall shirt and showed me how to stuff it down inside my new overalls. "Payday Best," I read on the bib. Agnes and Charles had taught me to read lots of words and I knew my ABC's.

Out the door and down the road we went, yelling to the dog, "Peggy, go home! You can't come."

I wasn't tired when I got to school, but I was kind of scared of all the kids. There must have been twenty of them, and some were big. The teacher was Miss Mabel Cox and she was very nice to me.

"Oh, you're Agnes' little brother. You sit right up here by the window. Here's a nice chalkboard. Why don't you write down as many ABC's as you can

12

think of, and then we'll talk about it later. Edgar, if you have to go to the outhouse, raise your hand like this and Charles or one of the older boys will take you out there."

When she said that, some of the boys snickered and someone whispered loudly: "Agnes has gotta baby. Teacher has gotta pet!"

Sitting at my new desk, I wrote down all my letters the way I had seen Agnes and Charley do it, and the way Mom and I had practiced. I never had to go to the outhouse, so I just sat and watched the teacher talk to the bigger kids. She had them sit up on the front row and she talked to them the way Reverend Boatman talked in church. Some kids didn't seem to like school, and one big boy cried when he couldn't answer any of the teacher's questions. I was glad that it wasn't me.

School didn't last very long that day, but, I thought it was pretty good anyway. The teacher had bragged on my ABC's and had given me a reading book.

We were walking home across the fields toward Grandpa's house where we would turn down the dirt road to our shack on the hill. I could hardly wait to tell Mom and Dad. Agnes and Charley were walking ahead and a big boy, B. J., was walking behind us. Suddenly, a wet hand hit me in the back and almost knocked me down. I reached back and my hand came away with a purple color all over it. Pokeberry juice! I could feel the wet of squashed berries running down my back. What would Mom say when she saw my new shirt! "Pokeberries!" I yelled. "He smeared berries all over my shirt." And I started to cry.

B. J. said, "He's such a baby!"

But that was about all he got out of his mouth. Charley was on him with both fists flying. I stopped crying and watched Charley chase B. J., who was now running for home, his nose bleeding down the front of his shirt.

Charley ran him all the way to Grandpa's property corner, while Agnes and I tried to catch up. When we did, B. J. had gone over the hill to home, but there was Grandpa Imhoff holding Charley by his overall straps.

"The Lord don't like boys that fight. I'm going to haf to take a belt to you, Charles."

Agnes said, "Grandpa. He was just fightin' because B. J. ruined Edgar's new shirt."

Grandpa eased his grip a little, but he still looked like he was going to do something.

By then, Grandma Imhoff had come out of the house and she was mad at Grandpa, not Charley. "You turn that boy loose this instant! B. J. deserves what he got. You are not goin' to whip your grandson."

We dragged ourselves up the hill. Mom almost fainted when she saw my shirt. "Lansakes!" she said. "Pokeberry juice is the hardest thing in the world to wash out. Well, Edgar, how did you like the first day of school?"

I am in a research review committee meeting in a university. We are in the tedious process of giving away money. Several of the deans of the university are present—to defend their turf. A researcher applicant is babbling like a child: "My colleague

and I . . . particularly from the point of view of . . . ah, trade-off mechanics . . . " He continues—faltering, stammering in an affected tone: "My last paper shows that er . . . the probablity index is not sensitive to manipulation in ah . . . the . . . er. . . ."

While the VP for research nods away, I begin to write a poem about my childhood. The speaker, observing my activity, looks pleased that someone would so industriously capture his words.

The Truth in 1936

If it is true that Mr. Reiman beats his wife with a
   buggy whip and works his horses to death,
It is also true that down in the woods the spotted
   salamander may be found now by turning over
   the fallen bark of the gum tree.
If it is a fact that the Qualls' boys cannot bring a
   lunch to school and can be seen to be starving,
It is a fact that last night the moon was so bright
   that we could pick out the old king oak tree way
   up on Waldbeiser Ridge.
If it is true that my daddy works on WPA and takes
   relief and never graduated from high school,
It is also true that he holds my hand when we walk
   and he whistles "My Blue Heaven."
If it is a fact that some children wear Sunday clothes
   every day and have servants to wait on them,
It is also a fact that we live on a windy hill where
   Mom and I fly a kite made from an old paper
   sack.
If it is true that we will probably never amount to
   anything, the odds being totally against such an
   event,
It is also true that we shall never forget the feel of
   hot dust squishing between our toes.

A short distance from the federal courthouse, I sit on a bench in Monument Circle in Indianapolis and try to gather my wits. I am unnerved from forty-five minutes on the witness stand in a district court case over the constitutionality of the federal strip-mine law. Not much fun being boss when you're also a defendant. The plaintiffs had a field day. Their six lawyers fed well on me and my (?) solicitor. We'll lose this one.

How on earth did I get into this situation? Why was I ever ambitious? Once, I had a great uncle who left Little Egypt and became an important man. His name was Wylie.

Uncle Wylie

When Dad told us to put on our school shoes, we knew for sure there was something awfully different about this day in August. Normally, we went barefoot until September. For another thing, it was not Sunday, yet Dad was here—not down at the coal mine. He was standing by the wash pan, fussing with a tie that Mom said he had borrowed from Uncle Ray.

We were all cleaned up. Yesterday Mom and Agnes had scrubbed out our overalls and washed their Sunday dresses with water that Charley and I had carried up from the branch—leaning away from opposite sides of the bucket so it wouldn't knock our knees.

And there was another funny thing about that

day: everyone looked good, but they didn't act very happy. Agnes complained about having to tie my shoes, "A second grader that cain't tie a bow knot!" She made me try to tie one by myself, so I had to run to catch up, with my shoe lace dragging as we headed down the hill to Mt. Joy Church to Uncle Wylie's funeral—whatever that was.

There were more wagons and cars in the church-yard than I had ever seen. Grandpa was right there to lead us into the church. He was looking very stern and he wore a black rag on his arm. We didn't sit where we usually did. It seemed like all us Imhoffs—all my relatives—were bunched together in the middle pews where the young people usually sat. Some people were crying. I had never seen any-one cry in church!

Reverend Boatman stood up and went over to a big, long box that had been placed by the cross. The box looked kind of like the big Pennsylvania trunk that Grandpa used for his best tools—only longer. Reverend Boatman placed his hand on the box and began to preach.

My mind wandered. Out a window of the church, I could see some red squirrels chasing each other up and down in the oak trees. Boy, they were having fun.

"Let him that is without sin cast the first stone."

The squirrels were out of sight. And a fly was on my head, but I dared not swat it.

"What is man that thou art mindful?"

Through a window I could see Grandpa's team tied in the shade. Old Bill, the mean horse from out West, was trying to bite the mare, Hazel. If I was out there, I'd get a stick and whack him.

"To everything there is a season, and a time to every purpose under the heaven. A time to be born, and a time to die . . . ashes to ashes . . . dust to dust."

17

With Reverend Boatman leading the way, my grandpa and uncles were carrying the long box out of the church. We kids followed Mom and Dad down the aisle. At the bottom of the church steps, Mom pulled me aside and whispered hard, "Edgar, you get yourself out to that outhouse and do your business, and hurry right back here! I don't want you a pinchin' yourself out in the graveyard."

I headed for the two-holer that stood at the edge of the woods. On the way, I heard two men talking by a wagon.

"No, Bill, I ain't goin' to the graveside. We ain't never buried a person here that kilt hisself!"

"Now, Frank, you ain't sure that Wylie Imhoff did that."

"Well, who else was in that jail cell, Bill?"

When I got back to the steps, I tried to ask Mom some questions, but she scolded me for not buttoning my overalls and hurried me off to join Dad, Agnes, and Charley in the graveyard.

Then we were walking slowly toward the box that stood by a big hole in the ground. The lid was open. My heart pounded and I wanted to run away. Reverend Boatman had said that Wylie was going to be turned into ashes. I didn't want to look in the box, but just ahead of me Agnes and Charley did look, so I turned my head.

I saw a handsome man in a dark suit . . . asleep in the August sun.

*I have just written a good check having six
figures left of the decimal. The broker scans the
check casually and, without fanfare, hands it to a
clerk for processing. The broker says, "Have a good
day," but he doesn't seem especially headed for one.
Come to think of it, neither do I.*

The Lord's Money

It was out at Mt. Joy, when we lived in the shack
on the hill. We three kids came running home early
from school. As we crossed the bridge over the
branch, Agnes was already yelling, "Mom, we got
let out of school to go to the circus! Everyone is
goin'! Can we go, Mom? We have a ride!"

Mom heard us right away because she was out in
the yard scrubbing clothes in a washtub. She stood
up drying her hands on her apron, looking at us
and not saying anything.

Then, "Wal, kids . . . I don't know . . . I don't see
how."

Agnes was not to be put off. We pressed close to
her when she said, "All the other kids are going!"

Mom looked awful sad, and we dared not think
too much about the reason behind that look.

"Okay, kids," she said, "we'll go down and see
Julia Graff."

We all hurried a half-mile down the dirt road.
Mom said, "Wait outside. Maybe Julia can help us."
When she went inside, we ran up beside the house
and listened by the open window.

Julia was apologizing, "Oh, Pearline, we just don't

have it. You know we'd loan you anything we had—but, we're as poor as Job's turkey."

Mom's voice was quavering, "Julia! I just don't have the heart to go out that door and tell them little kids they can't do what others do." (Agnes was covering her eyes and leaning up against the house. I felt a knot in my stomach.)

"Tarnation, Pearline! I know what! I got thirty cents of Sunday school collection here. The Lord is not usin' it right now. You return it when Ernie gets paid!"

We heard Mom heading toward the door, so we ran and stood in the middle of the yard, giggling. It was going to be a wonderful day. We were going to the circus!

President Carter is addressing an audience in a bill-signing ceremony in the Rose Garden. I am standing in the third file of people near him, just behind the sponsoring congressional members—maybe fifteen feet. I can see his facial expressions and hear his words without the aid of the amplifying equipment necessary to convey his message to the hundreds clustered down the lawn in the non-VIP territory. I suppose I should be impressed. (He seems like a good person.) As a speaker, however, this man is no Reverend Boatman.

The Reverend Boatman

I had an enormous advantage growing up where I
did, in Mt. Joy: I knew what God looked like. Why,
obviously, God looked like Reverend William Boatman, our pastor in the country church built by my
great-great-grandfather and other pioneers. God
was strong, ruddy in complexion, silver-haired, and
had fierce eyes that were always looking at you. I
didn't know about the blue serge suit and red tie,
but I was sure that if God came down to this earth
he would stand ramrod straight and proud like Reverend Boatman and his voice would ring out like a
bell as he offered heaven and threatened hell.

Everyone had a certain place in our church. Reverend Boatman expected to look up after his
opening prayer and see each person in the rightful
place. My Aunt Lillian's place was on the piano
stool. Men sat in the righthand pews—in winter,
old men sitting near the potbellied stove. Married
women sat in the lefthand pews—in winter, expec-
tant mothers sitting near the other potbellied stove.
The middle pews, between the two aisles, were
reserved for young folks. Couples "going together"
could sit in the rear center pews. Casual touchings
of hands—as when jointly holding a hymn book—
were allowed.

There were, however, no special indulgences for
fidgety little boys. Reverend Boatman expected me
and my kind to sit in the front row, almost at his
feet, and he expected us to listen.

Actually, it was not too difficult to listen to Reverend Boatman. The Bible and the Christian religion
came alive in that old country church.

In a Boatman sermon, David did not just "stroll
forth and cast a stone that went plunk on Goliath's
forehead." Oh no! David (Boatman) agonized and

feared and prayed to his God. Terrified, he approached this monster (Boatman) who roared with laughter so loud it hurt David's ears. David could smell the bloody sword and the gore of earlier victims on the man's clothing. David wanted to run away, to hide—do anything but fight this giant. "Oh Lord, save me from this beast!" And the Holy Ghost filled David's sling with a sharp rock (a gleaming crystal of quartz) and hurled it upward to lodge in the brain of the evil Goliath.

In the hot summer nights of a time later called the Great Depression, field-tired men listened as Boatman cast his spell. Careworn mothers in bonnets fanned themselves with funeral home fans, and listened. And down front, center, we little boys listened and believed that good does overcome evil, that the devil wants a Mt. Joy Lutheran (especially little boys and girls) more than anything in the world, and that heaven does await the faithful—in the sweet bye and bye.

I am one of those who still remembers and—down deep—believes that it could happen again.

Taking Relief

When we heard the car stop at the bottom of the hill and the loud whistling begin, we ran to tell Mom, "The relief man's comin'!" She was scrubbing clothes on a washboard and acted put out, "That ole Bill Roscoe. He comes at the durndest times!" Wiping soap on her apron, Mom followed us around to the front of the shack.

The relief man was coming up the hill with a big sack on his back. Mom sent Agnes to the creek for a bucket of water. Charley and I hung around to see the relief man empty his sack.

"Here's the pancake flour you asked for, and here's the prunes I forgot last time." He put down the cans and little sacks like they were eggs that would break. "Oh, Pearline! Before I go, why don't you set down and I'll tell you a funny story on the Qualls family." Mom looked like she'd rather get back to her washing, but she sat down.

"Well, a couple of weeks ago I took some of them Florida grapefruit to the Quallses for them to try out—the government gave us a whole boxcar load. I went back over there yesterday and asked Mrs. Qualls how she liked the grapefruit. You know what she said, Pearline? She said, 'Grapefruit? Grapefruit? Is that what you call them things? Lordy, I've baked 'em, fried 'em, and boiled 'em—and my boys still won't eat 'em'."

The relief man was laughing and slapping his legs and pounding on the step. Mom just sat there not laughing a bit.

"Well, these are hard times, Mr. Roscoe. A person might say or do just about anything. I do thank you for the relief food, but Lord, I wish we didn't have to take it."

Mr. Roscoe folded his empty sack and walked quietly down the hill. Mom and Agnes went back to scrubbing clothes. Charley and I went into the woods and sat in an old car body, pretending that we were sailing the ocean in a great ship.

_____

23

My psychologist friend advises that sons tend to deify their fathers. Yes, that is so. I still cannot think of him as quite human, although God knows he has given me enough chances. He sits before me now as an ill, old man intent on a crossword puzzle. I observe how carefully he works the puzzle: as if he is still marking plans for steel to be set and concrete to be poured.

I'm sure that he would love to look up and see again a hard-hatted superintendent of trades, come to seek and follow the orders of "The Old Man" (as he was always called when he was a project engineer). Sorry, Dad, I don't put up buildings—never could have. But, I will try to construct a word image of the remarkable thing that you did—of the extraordinary step that you took to change our lives and our fortunes.

Dad

Dad never liked our living in the shack. When he would leave in the morning, to hike to one of his pick-and-shovel jobs, he would hug Mom tight and say: "Bye, Hon. Don't you worry. We'll do better. I'll git us out of this shack someday." If Dad couldn't get a ride from work—which was most times—he wouldn't arrive home until we kids were in bed. But sometimes in the night I would wake up and see him by the light of a kerosene lamp. Dad would be sitting at our eating table, reading and putting marks on paper with the shiny pens and pencils Mom said cost a month's wages. And I would know that he was working on his correspondence school lessons—because Dad and Mom had talked a lot about it—the American Correspondence School, which Dad said was way up in Chicago.

I would lie there and watch him. Without removing his eyes from the papers on the table, Dad would push back his chair, roll a cigarette, and talk to himself while he smoked, "Well, I'll be doggone . . . if that ain't the darndest problem!" Then he would lean over the table again, and I would fall asleep to the sound of lead scratching on paper.

Mom had to go away to a hospital for awhile, but Dad kept working days and studying nights. Grandpa said, "Oh, he'll never finish!" But the lamp kept burning in the night. Snug in bed with Agnes and Charley, I would awake sometimes on a winter's night to the sound of Dad stamping his feet in the cold shack as he worked on.

About once a week the mailman brought a letter from the correspondence school. Grades! Mom would share with us Dad's high marks and read and reread the occasional few precious words of praise from some teacher Dad had never seen.

Dad's successes in school did not lead right away to a better job: three years after he began, he still walked five miles to work and carried groceries home in a towsack. But he built a picture frame for his first engineering certificate and kept on studying—he said—for a state registration examination that he would take, someday. Grandpa said, "Waste of time and money . . . should have stayed a farmer."

One evening Dad was late coming home to the shack. A violent thunderstorm was sweeping in from the west, already blowing limbs from the trees. Mom stood at the window to look down the road. "Oh, Ernie," she prayed. "Git here while you can!"

We kids joined her at the window peering out into rain and hail for some sign. Then, by the lightning flashes, we saw a lone figure marching up the road—sack on his back. "Dad!" On he came through the terrible storm. Before he even stepped through the door and into Mom's arms, I knew that he was safe and I felt that nothing could stop him.

That spring Dad got his first job in engineering, and we moved away from the shack on the hill.

_____

The Nolte Place

Agnes, Charley, and Edgar Imhoff, Nolte Place, circa
1938. This photograph was taken and hand-colored by
an itinerant photographer who was paid with four fry-
ing chickens.

The last time I went to visit my father,
in his hospital bed . . .
It had been a good flight from the West Coast,
lots of snow on the Wasatch, and Wyoming
passing by cold and lonesome.

The last time I stroked my father's
surgically shorn hair . . .
Other watchers were there in the room,
and they told interesting stories about old times,
Aunt Mabel declaring that Momma had wanted
    her to marry my father, and not Pearline,
"That's what Momma had said."

The last time I held my father in my arms,
helping the nurse to help him, I heard
my daughter, Kat, out in the hallway
talking horses with Joanne, and
I could just see these beautiful young women
riding down a trail—auburn hair bobbing like
    manes.

The last words I heard my father say,
I remember more the painful way he said them:
"Oh, oh, my Lord! . . . Oh! Oh! My Lord!"
And I wondered by whose authority we conduct
    such agony.

The Nolte Place
(1937)

Dad borrowed Uncle August's truck to move us to the new place. He loaded our stuff in back and had us crawl in on top, while he and Mom rode up front. We were so excited that we almost forgot the dog, Peggy, who was off chasing something in the woods. But Dad waited while we called her in, and now she sat with us on the truck headed down the dirt road toward town.

For days we kids had been asking Dad and Mom to tell us what it would be like at the new place. At first, they told us lots of things but lately they just said "shut up" or "wait and see." Crunched together in the back of the truck, we started up again—going over what we had heard, what had been promised.

"Edgar, Mom said you and Charley will have your own room."

"Is she teasin', Agnes?"

"No. And we're going to have a milk cow, and maybe goats . . . and, of course, chickens."

"I get to feed the chickens!"

"Okay—and Charley can milk the cows. You'll have to, because I'm going to help Mom can lots and lots of food. Dad says we're goin' to have a big, big garden."

"Agnes, will we really have lots and lots to eat . . . from now on?"

"Sure. Dad promised!"

We talked about how good school would be and how Mom had said we might see a motion picture show—which made us squeal at the thought.

The truck turned into a wide gravel road, went up a long grade, and began to slow down. Through the sideboards of the truck, we saw a white house that was at least three times the size of the shack—and there were trees blooming pink and white. We kids didn't say a word to each other. I know I was praying, "Oh, let this be the place that Dad promised."

And the truck did turn into a driveway by that house and stop in a big yard.

"Okay, kids! This is the Nolte Place. You can git out now but don't run off. There's a railroad track right down there. Trains run on it all the time. Be careful you look out and don't git run over."

Agnes and Charley and I were already running for the barn, which we saw would hold lots more than one cow. Then we ran out in the fields and counted the fruit trees (twenty!). We ran back to the house and pumped a drink of water from our well, after Dad showed us how to prime the pump (no more carrying water up a hill!). Finally, we ran around to the front porch and found a long wooden swing hung by chains fastened to the porch ceiling. We piled in and before long we were swinging so high that we could see the tops of houses, way off in Murphysboro. It sure looked like a lot of promises were going to be kept.

For the umpteenth time, my daughter asks me to write a story about "the time the fairies sang." I say, "Come on! You're twenty years old and still believing in fairies? Besides, William Allen White already wrote that story."

I acknowledge again that, yes, the fairies once did sing for me — on an enchanted night in spring.

Still, that is a story I will never write. My daughter persists. "All right," I say. "I'll tell you a true story about another mystery, but I want you to understand in advance that mysteries can be very troubling."

The Yellow Ball

My folks seldom threatened, "The bogeyman will get you!" Instead they would say, "We'll give you to the gypsies," or, "The gypsies will steal you if you don't watch out!" When we were very young, either remark would cause us to mend our ways. Because, in the summer, gypsies would wander, occasionally, along even the back roads of Jackson County, looking for odd jobs or some opportunity to sell a craft or to tell a fortune. Once, when we kids were playing by the roadside, a wagon pulled by handsome horses stopped by us, and the driver, a dark, wild-eyed man (we told Mom), tried to talk to us. We ran into the woods and headed for home as fast as we could get there.

When I was home with the chicken pox—but not very sick—it was not a wagon but an old beat-up truck that putted into the driveway of the Nolte Place. I stood in the shadow of the barn and watched the truck and its occupants with growing suspicion. The high bed of the truck was covered with canvas that was hooded at the back, forming sort of a house. When the driver got out and walked toward our back door, I could see that, yes, he was a gypsy. I guessed that was his wife in the truck, a dark woman with a red cloth around her head.

Mom and Peggy stopped him about halfway. The gypsy bowed and said, "Madame, do you have any pots that we can mend for you? . . . veery, veery good job, I promise you!"

"No, thank you," Mom said. "I'm about ready to throw mine away and git some new ones. They're beyond fixin'."

At that, the gypsy asked if he could see the pots, and Mom started making clear that she wasn't interested. I moved along the shadow of the barn to get a better look at their truck. Then, I saw him.

He had stuck his head out through a small hole in the back of the canvas hood and was looking right at me, trying to get my attention. I was shocked to see that his hair was blond and that his skin was white. His lips were moving like he was trying to whisper something to me.

I got scared and jumped farther back into the shadows. The boy's head ducked back inside the canvas hood. On the other side of the truck, I heard Mom's voice rising as she said she guessed she'd better "call my husband in from the pasture to tell you no!"

The boy's head appeared again, looking at me, and then he stuck out an arm. He was holding up a shiny yellow ball and seemed to be offering it to me—trying to draw me closer. He was smiling but looked scared. I know I was scared.

When the truck door slammed, the boy disappeared back behind the canvas. But when the truck pulled out of the driveway I could see a white face, back inside the canvas, looking out at me. I could feel his eyes on me all the way out to the road.

Mom had gone inside our house. I realized I just had to do something. I ran inside.

"Mom, Mom! They had a stolen boy in the back of that truck. Just like me! A boy just like me!" I went on and on.

Mom looked worried, grabbed me, and laid her wrist against my forehead to feel for fever. "Edgar, you don't feel like you got a fever. You'd better go lie down anyway. Lawzee me!"

I pleaded with her to listen to me. "Mom, it's all true!" And I told her and told her until I could see that she believed.

"Well, I don't doubt what you say. The thing is, what on earth can we do about it? Dad's not home and we don't have a car or even a telephone. Besides, no tellin' where that old truck has gone to by now."

It did not help ease my feelings when Charley came home from school and held up a shiny yellow ball, "Look what I found out on the road, just beyond our driveway."

In preparation for moving from Washington, D.C., I am in my office on a Sunday, sorting out things to keep from among hundreds of reports, publications, and file debris collected in years of service in the national headquarters. I am surprised at the ease of the task. Certain utilitarian objects are needed for the next job. Other than that, I decide to keep only things having an intrinsic value. Notwithstanding its fancy cover, a strategy briefing book warrants a quick flip into the trash can. But I extricate carefully from Scotch tape a weathered news clipping that quotes President Johnson, "Don't ever forget—a political capital is the poorest place to see and know what the people feel."

I also save a thank-you letter from a Wisconsin farmer (we actually helped a person). The priorities report that consumed every day for three months gets the deep six.

As the morning whiles away, I get innumerable little lifts of spirit with a toss here and a crushed file there. I decide to record the final score of the game using the scales in the mail room. It is: throwaways, 520 pounds; next job, 116 pounds; intrinsic value, 2 pounds.

Mr. Worthen

Old Mr. Worthen was out plowing corn when Charley and I crawled through his barbed wire fence to hunt for supper in his frog pond, which occupied low ground in the corner of the field. We were after the big green leopard frogs that squatted in the reeds bordering the pond. We caught several, and Charley killed them by holding the webbed feet and banging their heads against a fence post. The frogs shivered and were dead.

Mr. Worthen had always allowed us to enter his property, so we waved to him as he strode by driving a team of mules pulling a double-shovel plow. He was friendly enough, but we noticed he was limping, favoring the left leg. Charley said, "Let's ask him, when he comes around again, how he got hurt."

"Howdy, Mr. Worthen."

"How do boys." He pulled up the team and swept off his stained old hat to fan his face. "Catchin' supper?"

"Yessir, Mr. Worthen."

"That's good, boys. Make your ma happy."

"Uh . . . Mr. Worthen, how'd you hurt yurself?"

Mr. Worthen looked puzzled. "Don't knows as I did, boys. How come you ask?"

I turned away to probe in the plowed earth, but Charley persisted: "Well, you're favorin' your left leg."

Mr. Worthen laughed and slapped his overalls. "Well, boys these is hard times! I'm just savin' shoe leather."

Lifting his left foot, he showed a hole in the sole of a battered shoe, and a hole in the cardboard liner. "Been wearin' out this side long 'fore the other. Cain't afford to replace 'em. Gidup, Joe, Henry."

The people we once were,
we are not.

Field of clover,
Blue sky over.
"Apple core or
Baltimore,"
Moonlight bright,
Dogwood white.

The people we once were,
we are not.

But we were, my loves.
We were.

The Red Mittens

Uncle Ray's Buick was fine to ride to town in; there was plenty of room for Agnes and Charley and me on the back seat, and Mom and Dad sat up front with Uncle Ray. But, heck! We were still in that car now, and it was parked by a tavern—with Mom up front mad as a wet hen and us all hushed up in the back. Sure was a shame to waste a trip to town, especially a trip on a Saturday before Christmas!

There were lots of people walking up and down the street, carrying packages, and looking at the colored lights around every door and the tinsel edging all the windows. We watched them come by, people laughing and having a good time.

That's what Uncle Ray had said to Dad, when after one quick drive down the main street of Murphysboro he had pulled the car up by the tavern and jumped out: "Ernie, let's just have a short one! If a body cain't have a good time at Christmas, ain't no use in living. You don't mind do you, Pearline?"

Uncle Ray didn't wait to get an answer from our mom. He just hurried into the tavern.

Mom had hold of Dad's coat sleeve. "Ernie, that's about all I can stand of Ray's tricks. If you ain't back out here in a half-hour, I'll find someone to carry us home. Waitin' outside a tavern at Christmas!"

Dad acted hurt about the whole thing, "You won't haf to wait long, Hon. I'm goin' to see he has just one. He *is* my brother."

"Yes, Ernie! And these *are* your kids." And then Mom quit talking. Dad went into the tavern.

So, we sat there in a cold car, dying to jump out and wander up and down Main Street—but afraid to ask Mom, who was staring at the tavern like she could set it afire with her eyes.

Agnes saved us, even though it turned out she

37

was telling a fib. Right when Charley and I were beginning to feel sorry, Agnes squealed, "Oh, Mom! There's Doris Penrod from school. Can I go walk with her? Please, please!"

Mom always had a soft spot for her daughter. Mom was fair, too. No sooner than Agnes was on the sidewalk, Mom told Charley and me to "Git. But you be back here when that big clock at the drug store says eight o'clock! Hear?"

Oh, but Murphysboro was grand that night in the winter of 1938. We three hurried along Main Street, running from store window to store window—worshiping the mounds of sugar cones, the toys, the clothes. We began to play like we did when we all sat down under the cherry trees at home and looked at a new catalog.

"Agnes, I'm going to buy you that red dress," I said, as we pressed our faces against Penney's window.

"Well, thanks, Edgar. You can have those brown boots."

Down at Bower's Hardware, we "bought" Charley a Daisy air rifle. When we ran out of store windows, Agnes herded us across the street and we headed back by the Elks' building—some kind of lodge, Mom said. There, smack dab in the middle of the sidewalk was a big red Santa Claus standing by a box as big as our chicken coop. Kids were running up to him and, now and then, he would hand one of them a sack as big as a peck of potatoes. It was very exciting, and we stood there admiring him and almost believing in him.

Then he noticed us and said, "You kids in from the country?" (Now, how did he know that?)

"Yessir, we're from out by Number 5 School."

"Well, well (looking us over), how about some early Christmas!" And he handed each of us a sack and, to top it all, he handed me a pair of red mittens. We could smell the candy and feel the soft oranges and hard toys.

I don't remember how we got back to the car. We were just standing outside the car yelling, "Mom, Mom! Look what we got."

Mom turned around and she was crying. She rolled down the window and said, "Where in the tarnation did you get them things?" As Agnes told her, Mom began shaking her head slowly from side to side . . . but at least she stopped crying.

Agnes finished. Mom said, "You march right back down there and give them things back." We hugged our bags and didn't say anything. It seemed like an eternity passed before Mom said softly, "Wal . . . all right. Just this once. But you remember that we don't take charity any more. And don't you ever do it again. Git in the car. We got to take Ray home soon."

I found out that winter that with the red mittens I could make just as good snowballs as the other boys—without my hands freezing. And I kept the mittens long after they were of any practical use.

This high-ranking state official sitting confidently behind his big desk does not have to steal; that's what is so aggravating about it. His kids will not go hungry if he stops misusing federal funds. His wardrobe will not be downgraded from wool to nylon if he stops "accepting" monthly donations

from his employees. It is not that he lacks other means of making a good living. It's that even with all his good looks, education, and talent, he chooses to be this white-collar thief (who is about to run me out of his office). And it looks like he's going to get by with it.

'Bout Midnight . . . A Terrible Scream

On our walk home from school, we saw this truck coming slowly toward us alongside the gravel road. In the back of the truck a man was turning a big spool that unwound a thick cable that fell on the ground and lay there like a long black snake. We ran alongside the truck.

"Whatcha doin', mister?" we asked.

"I'm gettin' you kids some 'lectricity," he said. "Now, you won't have any excuse for not doin' your homework. You can have lights in your house and do lessons all night long." He laughed.

We told him we always got our schoolwork done anyway—well—maybe not Charley. We left and followed the electric cable until we turned into our driveway—the cable ran on toward town. Below our hill, some men were setting a big pole in the ground. Beyond them, the electric line was already fastened to other poles.

Mom was so excited she hadn't even made cookies. "Kids! We're goin' to have us electricity! Lawsee. I thought I'd be as old as Methuseluh 'fore I saw this happen. Thank the Lord this house was wired up before we ever moved here!"

We were glad that Mom was tickled and that even Dad was excited—already bringing home light bulbs and screwing them into empty sockets. "Now don't you kids mess around with these," he warned.

But we didn't have lights for quite a few days, because of what happened one night after the electric line had been fastened up on poles clear past our house.

I probably slept through most of the commotion that night, but I've heard about it so often it's like I was awake all the time. Mom always starts the story, "'Bout midnight, I heard this terrible screamin' comin' from out on the gravel road. It never did stop, though a car started up and tore out of here like blue blazes. I could hear that screamin' as long as I could hear that car headin' off toward town!"

Even I remembered firsthand what happened after that: the five of us were huddled together at the front window, peering out into the dark, wondering what on earth had happened.

On our way to school the morning after the screaming, we saw that part of the electric line was lying on the ground—cut and snarled. The men with the truck were there walking around and cussin'. We wanted to nose around but they yelled at us and shooed us on toward school.

When we came home for lunch, we saw a black car in our driveway. It had a gold star on the door: the sheriff! We went into the house and found a man sitting in the front room talking to Mom. He was holding a paper tablet on his knee and was writing as she talked.

"Ma'am, did you hear anything other than the screamin' and the car?"

"Wal, I heard some man talkin' . . . but I couldn't make it out, what with the screamin'."

"That was probably the other feller beggin' him to shut up. We think the one who fell from the pole was hurt awful bad, because we saw where he landed. Mighty high price to pay for stealin' copper wire worth jist a few cents a foot! Some people still desperate, I reckon."

The sheriff stood up to go.

"I thank you, ma'am. We'll catch 'em! Anybody hurt that bad has to go somewhere for doctorin'."

Mom didn't have lunch ready. She was fussin' around trying to heat up some butterbeans while we waited. "Oh, that poor man," she said. "I hope he don't have a family."

"The sheriff?" we asked. "No, silly! The one that fell off the pole," Mom answered.

A couple of nights later Dad came home from work and told us they had caught the man who had tried to steal the electric line—found him over in the Herrin hospital with a broken back.

That evening, Mom and Dad sat up and talked for the longest time about "that poor man," never once mentioning that he had been trying to steal.

The candidates for graduation from the School of Architecture are forming on the lawn in ranks of young men in morning suits and young women in white hats and dresses. Soon they will parade down the mall to receive their honors and degrees. Joking casually, yawning, and otherwise appearing nonchalant, they suffer the intrusion of photographer-parents who are intent on recording this moment in family history. "Oh, Dad . . . really! Don't you think we have enough?" I smile agreeably at my daughter but keep on shooting, because

I know there will never be enough images of this event. There are albums to be made for those who will never know what it is like to parade down a university mall in June, head held high with confidence that the future holds unlimited choices and rewards.

Pearline

We kids felt that moving to the Nolte Place was the best thing that had ever happened to us. It seemed that the world had been stretched way out and now held places of excitement—railroad trestles and brickyard ponds, fields for roaming, and even other kids to play with. And, we came home at noon for dinner and enjoyed Mom's cooking of the good things that we grew and raised on our land.

We would come running home from school about the time that Mom had tuned in a radio program that began with a preachy kind of voice that said, "Will the daughter of a poor miner, a girl from a little mountain town in Colorado, find happiness as the wife of England's richest lord? Stay tuned to this station."

We stayed tuned, because Mom really wanted to hear every word. No school talk (save that for after school). We were grateful for the hot meal at noon, so we just listened to the continuing story of the trouble this woman got into just because she married some rich guy.

Mom had changed since we had moved from the shack. Oh, it was hard to say just how or why. It didn't seem to be us (we hoped) and we knew it wasn't Dad, because right off he had bought a washing machine, and later, this radio. Dad was away at work most of the time, but that wasn't anything different from living in the shack. Sometimes Mom just seemed kind of sad.

We kids helped Mom all we could—doing most of

the outside chores—and, when she felt like talking, we listened.

Like all the Cagles, Mom was a great storyteller. She liked to talk while she was washing the supper dishes. We kids would gather round to feed scraps to the cat and to dry and put away dishes. Mom would stand at the kitchen sink and look out toward town and talk about her childhood. We found out that she was named after a soap once sold under the trade name of "Pearline" (poor Mom!). We heard things that weren't so good about men who drank and didn't take care for their families—like Grandpa Cagle before he quit drinking.

Most of Mom's stories were new, but there was one story she told lots of times. When she told it, she would stop washing dishes and just stand there with her hands in the dishwater, talking on and on.

The story was about how Grandma Cagle had finally insisted that Pearline deserved some education and had convinced Grandpa to get a paying job so Mom and her older sister could attend Brown's Business College in Marion. Mom would tell how she had studied "diligently" and received high marks and—unlike her sister, Mabel—had not flirted with the soldiers stationed on the square during the Williamson County mine wars. Mom explained the lessons she had mastered in English, shorthand, typing, and bookkeeping.

Most of the way through the story, Mom's face would be bright, but, when she got toward the end, it never was. We only asked her—one time, "Then what happened, Mom?" For, the answer had something to do with Dad and with us—and with life, I guess. No matter how many times she repeated the story that began "When I attended Brown's Business College . . . " we never once said, "Oh, Mom. We've heard that one before!"

Long before the Rocky Mountains were formed, the land now named Illinois was uplifted gently from the sea and added to the girth of the immature North American continent. Illinois has never attained any significant height, remaining always a broad pan-shaped cake of layered rocks—warped downward in its geographic center and blanketed with soil and sediment. Some of the layered coal and rocks, buried one thousand feet below the land surface in the middle of the state, are seen in the bluffs at the Mississippi River floodplain.

Before the glaciers came down from Canada to bury this cake of rocks under hundreds of feet of mud and gravel, it was not so easy for the rivers of interior Illinois to escape. Some ancestral streams were able to breach the rock rim of the basin and join the Mississippi and the Ohio rivers.

The southernmost rim of the basin, the Shawnee Hills, has remained a persistent barrier to streams. The Big Muddy and the Saline rivers, failing to penetrate the hills, have had to find a way around them.

With hills to the south, and big rivers on three sides, the southern part of Illinois—a triangular expanse of land that came to be called Little Egypt—has remained a place apart. Flora and fauna—including people—have been accepted somewhat reluctantly, but once rooted have been protected jealously from change and held in the bosom of the land.

45

In the Bosom of the Land

Charley and I had not intended to be late for
school, certainly not with this new teacher. We were
telling her, now, why we were late, pointing to the
mud on our shoes and explaining that the path
through the bottoms had been flooded. We told her
we finally had to turn back and take the roundabout
way through the field. But the teacher just looked
mad and said, "I don't want any of your excuses!
March right back outside and clean your shoes."

I thought once about telling her of the strange
snakelike creatures we had seen wiggling in the
flooded bottoms. They must've been the eels that
Uncle Clyde was talking about when he was telling
us how the Indians lived here before we came. But I
kept my mouth shut, cleaned my shoes, and hurried
in to the lesson.

Miss Stephens was standing up and yelling at us,
again. "Don't pronounce the word 'Ill-a-noise.' You
live in 'Ill-i-noy!' I am from northern 'Ill-i-noy.' You
live in southern 'Ill-i-noy.' "

It had been like that ever since January when she
had taken over for Mr. Burns, who had gotten sick.
Always talking that way to us.

"You do not live north of 'Karo. That is the name
of a syrup that people put on hotcakes. Pronounce
the word after me. 'Cairo.' Again, 'Cairo.' You must
not sound like hicks."

Even though the old teacher had paddled, we
missed him. Sometimes he had even played running games with us, like "Red Rover, Come Over."
And he had loved to talk about Indians. Charley
and I showed him our ax blades and spears, and he
really made a fuss over them. This new teacher just
talked about where she came from and how dumb
we were. When I told her that the wildflowers were
abloom down in the bottoms, she said, "You mean,

'blooming,' not 'abloom.' And Edgar, you need to do a lot more work on your fractions. You're not making enough progress."

This day, during recess, some kids started skipping an old barn rope. We began jumping in and out and singing the song:

Goin' down to Cairo, to Cairo, to Cairo.
Goin' down to Cairo to git my Liza Jane.
Black them shoes and amake 'em shine.
Howdee! Howdee . . .

Right then Miss Stephens came around the corner of the schoolhouse and grabbed that old barn rope. "You just won't learn!" she yelled. "Are you people down here stupid? I said, don't pronounce the word 'Karo!'"

That ended recess. We just slunk inside and tried to keep out of trouble the rest of the day. On the way home, Agnes said she was "goin' to tell Mom that the teacher called us stupid." Charley and I didn't even bother to look for arrowheads in the field, even though Clarence Evans had just plowed and there might be some. School wasn't a bit of fun.

Held a few days later, the last day of school ceremony did not amount to much. Oh, everyone brought lunches and we kids recited poems and stuff, but it was different. Almost no one talked with Miss Stephens. I overheard Mrs. Hall whisper, "I'll not say a word to that woman. She'd just think it was dumb."

That was the last we saw of Miss Stephens. Next fall, on the first day of school, we met a new teacher, Mrs. Robinson—from Carbondale. After she smiled and said hello, she held up a snakeskin and asked, "Who can tell me what this is?" Half the arms in school shot up. Why, anyone could tell that was a fresh skin from a copperhead—and a big one at that. It was going to be a good year.

Even in California, there is a remnant of what was—if you care to risk a walk before the dawn. The Sierras are still a dark mystery on the horizon. In these old oaks, who knows what cougar preyed? What bear waited?

A dark object crosses my path. I switch on my flashlight to expose a red fox. It gives me a yellow-eyed glare before trotting casually away.

Something Wild

One of the least successful men in my family was Clyde Evans, my uncle. Anyway, that's what I heard some grown-ups say. They said that he cut his hay too long and never cleaned his fence rows (of course, such people must not know about the meadowlark nests).

Charley and I didn't care what they said. The nice thing about Uncle Clyde was that he always had plenty of time. In fact, when we asked permission to cross the field from Grandpa's house, to visit our cousin David Evans, Mom would not let us leave Grandpa's until she figured Uncle Clyde was through milking. Because Mom knew that Uncle Clyde would just stop whatever he was doing and start telling stories—which he did this very evening.

"Well sir! Howdee! You boys are lookin' right smart. Right smart! Didn't see any snakes on the way here, did ya? Not lak it used to be." We sat down in the yard, because it looked like here was comin' a humdinger of a story.

"Back when the pioneers settled this country, the Kinkaid Bottoms was all covered with giant trees. Some of them early settlers, Jim Evans and your great-grandpa Andrew, cut a road from here into the bottoms so's they could haul out that timber."

"That road warn't much more than a path through the wilderness—there was lots of wild animals still here in those days. In the evenings, the men heard panthers screamin' at 'em. Guess them animals didn't like us messin' round with their woods!"

"Well, sir, . . . one evening, comin' home to Mt. Joy, Jim Evans saw a funny lookin' mark across the roadbed. He stopped the team of oxen and went up to take a look. There in the dust was a snake trail as wide as his foot was long! Why! A snake that wide must be all of twelve to fourteen feet long, and big enough to swallow a dog . . . or even a child."

"The next day—in broad daylight—some men tried to track that ole snake. But, long towards dark, their dogs got scared and wouldn't run no more, so they had to turn back."

We started to ask a dozen questions, but Aunt Lillian stepped out from the kitchen porch, carrying a lantern and yelling for Uncle Clyde: "Clyde? Clyde? Oh, there you are! What you doin' sittin' out here in the dark? You'd better git that milk separated before it sours. Boys, let him alone until he runs the separator!"

"Yes, ma'am." But we hung close to Uncle Clyde as he opened the screen door and headed for the separator with two pails of milk. I felt sweet relief when the door banged shut, closing us in the house.

There was something out there in the dark. I could just feel it. Maybe that old snake was gone, and the Indians, too, and the panthers. But there was still something wild out there, and I was glad that Dad had promised to drive by and pick us up, so we would not have to walk back to Grandpa's in the night.

When I see young men head off to one of our wars, I regret not so much what they will encounter overseas, but what they will leave behind. Most of them will return physically sound, but none of them will come back young. When I think about that, I recall one particular November day in 1950 at Fort Leonard Wood, Missouri, when a platoon of men sat in a semicircle of woods barren of leaves. We were not permitted to recline. The fall sun bore through the HBT jackets inducing drowsiness. Occasionally and inevitably, a soldier's back would contact the trunk of a tree causing him to recoil to a position more suitable to hear Captain Haislip declare, "Men, your mission here is to learn to kill, to kill effectively, and to survive in so doing."

Right at the high point of the Captain's training lecture—his swagger stick whipping the air—I heard wild geese calling and sneaked a look at them against the bluest sky you'll ever see. The geese were flying southeast—probably going to Horseshoe Lake for the winter.

The Lesson

The north field of the Nolte Place had gone to
weeds higher than a boy's head and too thick for
passage by all things except snakes, mice, our hungry old cat, and Charley and me. With an enterprise
common to older brothers, Charley had forced out a
narrow secret path through the acres of giant horse-
weeds and brambles. One minute, Mom would
glance up from the clothes washing and see that the
boys were indeed hoeing the garden. The very next
minute, Mom would look up again and we would
have disappeared, "poof," and she would think,
"Lawzee me . . . hope they haven't run off to that
brickplant pit or to the railroad trestle! A body can't
keep track of those boys."

It was Charley who kept track of us on the other
side of the field—leading us to daily adventures in
woods, creeks, berry patches, and straw stacks.
Never mind that the schoolteacher paddled Charley
for being a slowpoke and for daydreaming. Never
mind that Dad took a belt to him for laziness. I
knew my older brother's worth—and it exceeded
everyone's I knew, except Reverend Boatman's.

One evening, Charley and I were carrying in the
milk from the barn, when Dad drove in from his
town job. He parked the old Ford and came toward
us with a strange package under his arm. He
winked at us and said, "Got a surprise here for you
boys, but you got to wait until after supper." Then
he shut up, and during supper he didn't even look at
the box he'd placed on the mantle next to the Shirley
Temple pitchers. Between bites of potato cakes and
stewed tomatoes, Charley and I exchanged grins.

Sometime after supper, Dad finished his smoke
and called us to him. "Okay, boys. It's time you
learned something." He took down the box and

opened the lid. Since I was nearsighted, my face was almost in the box, so I was the first to see the maroon leather of two sets of shiny boxing gloves.

I jumped back a step and must have looked really surprised for Dad said, "Now boys, don't be scared. You got to learn how to fight." I guess I just went sort of numb because I don't remember Dad tying the big gloves on my hands. The first thing I remember is Charley coming toward me with hands as big as boulders. Then he hit me, but it didn't hurt where he hit me. It hurt me in the pit of my stomach. Dad yelled, "Get your hands up. Hit him back!" But I just stood there with the big gloves dangling at my sides. Under Dad's prodding, Charley hit me a few more times, and I became hysterical, sobbing and yelling, "I don't want to hit Charles. I don't want to hit him."

That boxing lesson ended the evening it began, in 1938. And we never again put on the gloves.

In the ambience of the time and place, we can scarcely avoid feelings of self-importance. We six newly appointed directors of a brand new federal agency sit high on the veranda of the Hotel Washington, sipping our drinks while looking out on the Mall and down on the White House. Reporters are hovering near our table, trying to catch our conversations, eager to record even casual remarks concerning the difficult mission we have accepted.

As night comes, our group is beginning to whoop it up. Now they can hear us!

I find myself withdrawing from the headiness of the moment—from the "loftiness" of our position—under a sense of foreboding that beyond the euphoria of this moment lies plenty of misery. I must have been about ten years old when I learned about the pain of being in charge.

The Goatmaster

Most of the promises that Dad made about the Nolte Place eventually came true. Shortly after we had moved in, Grandpa Imhoff drove his team into our driveway, with a big old cow tied to the back of the wagon. She was kind of bony, but her bag was so full of milk that it looked like it was about to bust. Grandpa said, "Here! You'd better see to this animal. I don't think she got milked this mornin'."

That first cow, Old Bird, gave us milk and calves right on schedule. Our cows were awfully good-natured and would put up with us swinging around their necks and even us riding them in from the pasture (but Dad better not see). We took good care of the cattle—treating them almost like they were people—except for a calf named Buster.

One night Old Bird decided to have another calf. Agnes and I held the lantern while Dad helped Old Bird with the delivery. Mom joined us just as the rear end of a calf was coming out. Mom said, "Now, kids, that looks like a bull calf. Don't you go makin' a pet out of him! We need us some beef for winter. And don't go givin' him a name, either!"

We tried to mind, but as he grew that calf became so playful and pretty that we couldn't leave him alone. We named him Buster.

One day after school, we didn't see Buster in the

pasture and asked Mom about him. "Wal . . ." she said, "Buster has been taken down to Aunt Blanche's." We asked if he was coming back. "Sort of. Tomorrow, I 'spect."

The next day we kids could smell meat cooking before we'd crossed the cornfield. When we walked into the kitchen, Mom pointed to a bunch of packages on the counter, and a big pressure cooker steaming away on the stove. "Kids, you might as well know—I'm cookin' Buster." Agnes screamed and ran from the house. I followed her into the barn where she stood gagging and crying. It was late winter before Agnes would touch a single morsel of Buster, but I weakened as early as Thanksgiving Day. You couldn't beat Mom's cooking—even if she had cooked up Buster.

Right after we had gotten Old Bird, and Charley had learned how to milk her, a stray cat showed up in the barn at milking time. Charley took one look at her sitting politely in the shadows and squirted hot milk right in her face. That cat did not budge an inch but just shut her eyes and started wiping her face and licking her paws like crazy. That's how we got Ole Puss to stay at the Nolte Place.

It was hard to tell the difference between our pets and our stock—especially with the goats. Uncle August brought the first goat to us in the back of his coal truck. When he untied her, she jumped down and ran up to Charley and butted him, hard. I went right over and she didn't do a thing to me but chew on her cud while I scratched under her chin. Right there Mom said, "I do declare! She likes you, Edgar. Then you'll be the goatmaster. You'll feed 'em, water 'em, and milk 'em. I'm putting you in charge. There'll be more goats."

Mom was right. We kept the first goat, Old Lulubelle, and always kept at least one kid—selling

54

milk and other goats on a regular basis. Goats took a lot of attention; they had to be tethered because none of our fences would hold them. But I didn't mind; I just plain liked goats. They were always nibbling at me or rubbing against me. At school I got teased that I smelled like a goat; but that was okay.

My favorite goat was a little nanny we named Linda Lou. She was born in the winter, so small that we kept her in the warm house—to improve her chances. Linda Lou, my dog Peggy, and a stray dog named Tiny (who came to us with a broken leg) would lie together in a lumpy pile, as near to the stove as they could get without singeing. Our radio was in that room. Mom soon learned to leave the radio on, because if it were turned off, Linda Lou would jump up and run around the house bleating. Then Peggy would start barking, which would cause Tiny to howl. Quite a mess for just a durned old radio program!

Linda Lou never did grow up, although she soon got too big for the house and was jumping on top of tables and beds. We put her out with her mom, Lulubelle, where she did just fine—until I got sick.

When I got sick, Charley took over the care of the goats, and, I guess, he just wasn't cut out to be a goatmaster—no one's perfect. Mom said that if Charley hadn't given Linda Lou all that green fodder, she wouldn't have swelled up and died like that.

I was awful mad at Charley until I saw that he was as near to crying as he ever gets, so I stopped blaming him—after awhile. If I hadn't gotten sick. . . .

I'm the one who buried Linda Lou. Mom said that was part of the job of being a goatmaster.

55

The Chevrolet has cost us $125. It is not worth it. The brakes fail on a hill in Missouri, one of many mechanical failures that slow our odyssey. We sleep in a fence row too close to a small town and are rousted out by the local police. We swear silently and leave, forgetting the insult within a mile or so. After we cross the brown Missouri River, the communities begin to stretch out and the land to step up. Trees disappear except along the muddy shallow streams. We stop to cool the engine and to walk up a sand hill through tall grass bending to a stiff wind. Far on the horizon a thin blue line with a white top fills all the western margin of the sky: first glimpse of the Rockies. Stopping for gas, we are asked by an old man with a limp, "You boys going to the mountains? Wish I was."

Winding Up A Dream

The Nolte Place held mysteries that we kids never solved. There were the long-necked dark green bottles that we found way back in the basement wall— rows and rows of them, stoppered and smelling sour and moldy. Mom said that she wouldn't have that stuff in the house and made us haul the bottles into the field and bury them in a gully. We asked what they were. Dad only said, "Don't worry about what the last people here did. Just mind your own business."

Then there was the attic we kids got into one day when Mom and Dad had gone to town. We put an orchard ladder on the front porch and Agnes pushed up the door that had been hung in the porch ceiling. She yelled down, "There's all kinds of stuff up here!" When Charley and I climbed up to join her, we saw that was not quite true. There sure was a lot of dust, but only two boxes and what looked like a piece of furniture.

One of the boxes contained some old-fashioned clothes and a soldier's uniform we guessed was from World War I. The left sleeve was folded and pinned against the side of the jacket. Later we asked if that meant the Germans had shot his arm off." But Mom and Dad didn't have an answer.

We had more luck with the other box and the furniture. The box was full of phonograph records and the "furniture" turned out to be a Victrola on legs. We talked Dad into bringing it down from the attic, promising over and over that we would not play it during the week and that playing it would not interfere with our chores or with school. And we agreed that Sunday was for church, certainly not for loud music. That left only Saturdays, and because there were always outdoor chores—only rainy Saturdays.

Because of the Victrola, waking up to a rainy Saturday became a special treat. After we had fed the animals, we kids would gather in the living room and begin sorting through the dozens of old phonograph records that had been brought down from the attic. We would take turns cranking the windup spring that turned the records, and in selecting one to play. Charley liked best "The Wreck of Old Ninety-Seven," a song about a train engineer who bravely stayed at the controls of his runaway engine, allowing his crew to jump to safety, while he "with his hand on the throttle was scalded to death by the steam." Charley said he was going to be a railroad man.

Agnes' favorite record was "The Blue Danube Waltz." Holding the hem of her cotton dress, she would glide around the living room, asking us, "How do I look? Can't you just see me at a ball?" We thought she was a pretty dancer.

We played all the records but the one that set me to dreaming was "Billy the Kid." As much as my small size would allow, I demanded silence and a fresh windup of the Victrola before I placed the record gently on the turntable and lowered the steel needle to hear the story of a young man who ran free and wild "out in New Mexico, many years ago."

There was hardly a rainy Saturday that I didn't hear: "In Old Silver City, he went to the bad . . . at the age of twelve years he killed his first man." Round and round the record would turn unraveling the tale that led up to "his sad end."

I was never bothered by the fact that his best friend, Sheriff Pat Garrett, shot Billy dead. No, I was just enjoying riding around in the canyons and mountains, free and wild, dressed in black, carrying a big pistol—slung low, feared and envied by grown men. Heck, it sounded like Billy got to do that for quite a while—maybe ten years. And ten years was a long, long time.

A couple of years after Grandma died of cancer, Grandpa dropped dead. I was thousands of miles away and couldn't return home for the funeral. I hope that just once in a while, in his loneliness,

58

*Grandpa thought of the little boy who made big talk
and rode proudly beside him on the wagon hauling
cream to town.*

Cream to Town

One of Grandpa Imhoff's few cash crops was
cream from his milk cows. Grandpa hauled the
cream to town every Saturday, driving a horse-
drawn wagon along a dirt road leading from the
Kinkaid Hills to Murphysboro. Sometimes I would
ride with him. The road ran past the house of
Grandpa's brother, Andy — my great uncle. We never
stopped there. As the eldest son, Uncle Andy had
inherited a big white house and red barn, and rich
farmlands that made Grandpa's crops look puny. As
a younger son, Grandpa had gotten a small hill
farm and some stock.

I was always so impressed with the abundance of
Uncle Andy's place that I would comment favorably
every time Grandpa and I passed by. Grandpa never
said a cross word about my oohing and ahhing, but
he would sort of whip up the team so that we didn't
linger on that part of the trip.

I never told Grandpa that I was glad to be his
grandson and not Uncle Andy's, but I was. Grandpa
was tall and broad-shouldered, and as hard and lean
as a hickory stick. He had deep brown eyes that
could bore right through you. Mom said that
Grandpa made people nervous just looking at them.
Maybe, but I'm sure he couldn't help it. I saw Uncle
Andy in church, a few times. He looked fat and soft.
I thought, "If that is what a silver spoon in your
mouth does to you, I'd rather be like Grandpa."

Until Grandpa moved to town to retire and die,
he never had electricity. Sometimes Charley and I
would help him separate his cream by turning the

big hand-propelled centrifuge that crowded his back porch. Once you got it started, it was easy to turn, emitting a high-pitched droning sound that spilled across the countryside: "Umm-ummuh-umm-ummuh," announcing nightfall in Mt. Joy.

After separating the cream, we boys were free to sit and read by a kerosene lamp. By that time of the evening, Grandpa had already worked twelve to fourteen hours. But, he was always interested in what we were reading and once surprised us by being able to work a hard math problem.

Grandpa said that he couldn't afford doctors. He treated himself, whatever the problem, curing blood poisoning with mullein-leaf packs and colic with sugared kerosene.

After Grandpa moved to town, he lived fewer years than a person of his vigor and ancestry should've. I suspect that he didn't like living where he couldn't see hills and creeks. Every spring, Grandpa planted his whole backyard in potatoes and sweet corn, making a big fuss over bringing in a "hired man" to plow the back half of the town lot.

When Grandpa wasn't limping around in the backyard, he could be found sitting on the front porch reading. He liked stories about faraway places.

Traveling at 600 MPH we cross the once Great Plains in one hour, transcending a broad range of ecology, agriculture, and attitudes. We jet from

arid to humid, from natural brown to irrigated green to the dark green woods of southern Illinois. Yes, they are down there somewhere, because we just crossed the Mississippi; and there is the Wabash River and the Ohio. As the miles disappear, we are comfortable with our beverage and meal service, sitting in a plush lounge in a sterilized, pressurized cabin. Below us the light begins to fade. There is not much that can be discerned in the present; but, I see the past clearly . . . clearly.

The Bum

The bum was sitting on the slab of concrete that covered our well. He was enjoying the potato soup, bread, and buttermilk that Mom had served him. He had braved Peggy's furious barking and her bared teeth and had stood defenseless by the back door, his hat in hand . . . waiting for the lady of the house to appear.

Mom had come to the door about the same time that I had dropped my hoe and walked over from the garden. I heard him say what most of the bums say, "Mornin', ma'am (bowing his head). Have you got some work I could do for somethin' to eat? I'm awful hungry."

He was somewhat dirty, stained with coal dust, but his clothes were better than rags and he wore a trimmed beard. He was carrying a tow sack of "things"—probably the pans, grub, and old clothes that most bums carried to make their camp.

Mom had looked at him a little while before deciding that he was okay. (She almost never turned anyone away.)

"Wal . . . the kids do most of the work around here. But, I'd be glad to share what we got. You sit

61

down over there by the pump and I'll fix somethin'. By the way, you ain't ever run across an Edgar Wallace in your travels—blue eyes, probably white hair by now?" (Mom almost always asked the bums about my namesake, Uncle Ed.)

The bum had taken in the question and really thought about the name. "Edgar Wallace? . . . No, ma'am, I haven't. But there's an awful lot of us out there (motioning toward the railroad tracks). I do thank you for the food."

Now, he was through eating and was lining up the glass, spoon, and bowl in the open so we could see clearly that he had not taken them and was grateful for the food. I watched him from the garden. He walked to the railroad embankment that began right behind our barn. Then he sat down in the sun and pulled what looked like a book from his tow sack.

I was curious and had to go back there anyway to dump a wagonload of rocks that I had dug up hoeing.

He heard me coming, but didn't look up from his book until I asked: "Whatcha readin'?"

"What grade are you in, boy?"

"Fourth grade, . . . sir."

"Well, I doubt if you're reading this kind of stuff, son. This is the last of the books from my store. It's by a famous man who lived long ago. His name was William Shakespeare."

"Oh." (I had never heard that name.) "Is it funny or sad?"

He laughed. "Well, son, it's kind of like life nowdays. Some of both. Here comes my train. Be good to your mother, boy."

I watched him pull up on a coal train headed west on the Iron Mountain Road.

Betty and I have flown to Illinois so that—as a new wife—she can meet my relatives. The visit to Marion is going rather well. The Cagles have been taken with her Norwegian looks and Minnesota manners; she has been captured by their warm hospitality and southern accents.

The second morning, we come to the breakfast table to find the usual fare of biscuits and gravy and cornmeal mush.

"What is this?" Betty asks, somewhat imploringly upon sight of the little arms and legs being loaded on her plate by proud Grandpa Cagle.

"Haw! Haw! S'prised you! I were out in the woods at the crack-a-dawn, awaitin' for them squirrels. They ain't as many as they used to be—but I shot you a mess anyway. Nuthin' like young squirrels that hain't cut their nuts yet!"

And my eighty-year-old grandpa all but dances around the kitchen to show his delight in still being able to bring meat into the house and to astonish a beautiful young lady. Out the corners of my eyes, I see that Betty is already looking for an opportunity to slide some of the fried things onto my plate.

The Squirrel Hunter

I was in my twenties before I discovered that Grandpa Cagle could not write his own name—that he was illiterate. Oh, he could cipher enough to carpenter—very able at building—but he had never learned letters. It was Grandma who told on him.

She was writing to me when I lived in New Mexico. I told her that I appreciated her letters but sure would like it if Grandpa Vince added a note. Next time she wrote, she said, "Honey, don't you know that your Grandpa can't even write his own name? I do all that for him."

It was a credit to his intelligence that he had been able to hide that from me. When I read Grandma's letter I recalled how—when I was a little kid riding around on his coal deliveries (he had just gotten the job)—Grandpa challenged me to read to him the street signs and road signs, saying: "Okay, boy! Let's see what they are teachin' yuh in 'at school. What's that sign say?"

Grandpa said that his people came from the Little Pigeon River Country of the Great Smoky Mountains. His grandpap liked the forests of southern Illinois and cleared only enough for corn and melon, leaving the rest of the woods for the squirrels and passenger pigeons. When the pigeons came no more and the soil washed thin, they made do as best they could with laboring, teamstering, and coal mining—which became a major activity in Little Egypt in the middle of the nineteenth century.

At age nine, Vince began to work in the shallow coal mines of Williamson County as a "pony boy." He cared for the mules kept underground to pull coal cars.

Grandpa seldom talked to me about those days. His stories never dwelt on his own miseries. But, after his death, Grandma Cagle said that at the age of twelve years he became a "crawl miner." A crawl miner works a seam of coal so thin that he has to lie on his side or work on all fours, because of the low roof. (You can't stand erect in a crawl mine.)

At sixteen, Grandpa's back was broken in a roof fall, bending him for the rest of his days but probably adding years to his life because the injury made him unfit for underground mining.

He was a devil-may-care, wiry little man who sparkled when he talked, and he talked almost endlessly, delighting his grandchildren with stories of the backwoods and of the outlaws who frequented Little Egypt. He may have stretched the truth a bit, but we children had no inkling of that as we sat with the men on drowsy Sunday afternoons through the 1930s while they smoked and talked and talked.

When Vince went into one of his spellbinders, he caught the attention of the men and the kids present:

Now (pointing his Barlowe knife at an imaginary face), Hosie Cagle got hisself mixed-up with a high-falutin' woman from Paducah. Had to have the dough to squire her for she was some looker! (spitting tobacco on a tree) Hosie came to me and sez: "Vince, let's us make some liquor down in your woods!" (laughter by the men) I sez, Hosie, my Pap darn near got kilt fur that . . . count me out (murmur of agreement) Hosie was rat put out and he sez: "Stay poor and see's if I care!" Next I hear, Hosie is a runnin' with the Berger gang an' (pause to look around) he and that Paducah woman is a driving aroun' in a big old Buick lickety-split down the hard road. Wal, that went along for a spell, then the Shelton boys got mighty tared of Hosie a hornin' in on their booze business. They tried to scare him off, but Hosie paid no mind (heads nodding agreement). Then, one night, Hosie was a drivin' like a bat out of hell, down the hard road to visit that Paducah woman . . . spect he never did see the steel cable that had been cinched across the Herrin road, just about Adam's apple high to him asittin' in his Buick. They knowed Hosie was a 'comin and (bold stroke with the knife on a stick) they cut his head off slick as a pistol.

My older brother lives in the Midwest. He has worked for one firm for over thirty years. Never married, he will occasionally bundle up his laundry and take it home to our mother, who lives in a small town downstate.

One does not drive laundry two hundred miles for any practical reason. I would guess that he just goes home for the "company," and the laundry conceals the loneliness. My kid brother, Mike (who was born after I had left southern Illinois), and his family and my older sister and her family are down home a lot. They eat a lot of chicken and apple pie and engage in slow talk out on the screened-in porch. Sometimes when I get lonesome in the many airports and motels, I think of them.

I wonder — when my older brother goes home — does he ever go back to the secret place that we made in the woods, out of a storm-fallen tree and a lot of imagination? I like to think of him in that place: sitting up front of me astraddle the trunk, our legs pushing off the ground in a rhythmic gait as the tree bounced up and down, hung by its roots in the Illinois soil, mounted by two small boys headed West on its prostrate limbs.

We never revealed that secret place. Sometimes when we were supposed to be hoeing, or berry-picking, or watching the goats, we would slip off and lead a wagon train through shining mountains or save a beautiful girl from evil men. Bouncing up and down in the quiet woods on that old tree, we rode through the summer of 1939, 1940, *and maybe even 1941. Then we were growing up, and the war was coming, and everything was changing, forever.*

Sometimes I wish that I had a secret place like that, today. My older brother would tell me the plot, and we would mount up and ride off to do noble deeds in a simple world.

The Sneedham Girls

From his perch high in the wild cherry tree, Charley saw the big black car coming down the road toward the Nolte Place. He knew it was an especially big car, because of the size of the dust cloud it was causing. By the time the car slowed to turn into our place, Charley had already shinnied down the tree. We ran into the house to tell Mom and Agnes.

Mom was not particularly pleased to have her canning interrupted. Wiping berry juice on her apron, she led us outside to see what all the fuss was about.

Aunt Marie was getting out of a car that was as big as my uncle's coal truck. "Hi, Pearline. I'm sorry to drop in on you like this . . . I just had to see ya. Kin you talk for awhile?"

"Why sure, Marie," Mom said. "Come in an we'll talk while I finish them berries. And who's this, Marie?" Mom showed her good manners by not forgetting there were three people left in the big automobile.

Marie introduced the driver of the automobile. "This is Fred. He's Mr. Sneedham's chauffeur. Fred, this is my sister Pearline and her kids. Pearline, it was awful nice of Fred to bring me out here from Murphysboro. We got to wait most of the afternoon for Mr. Sneedham to inspect his shoe factory. Then, we're drivin' back to St. Louis."

Mom smiled in at Fred. "That sure is nice of you. You set down over there in the shade in that rocker. I'll bring you a nice piece of berry pie and a glass of cold milk."

When Fred got out of the car, our eyes almost bugged out: he was wearing a uniform like a soldier. He did just what Mom said and went over and sat beneath the catalpa tree.

By then, Marie was opening the back door of the automobile. "Girls, would you like to come out and see a real farm? It'll be for just a little while . . ." Two girls, one about Agnes' age (eleven) and one Charley's age (ten), stepped daintily from the enormous back seat.

"Pearline . . . kids, this is Madeline and Caroline. That's who I look out for at the Sneedhams."

Agnes, Charley, and I could not have said a word if our lives depended on it. We stood there, our mouths open, gawking at the sight. Not even in the Sears catalog had we ever seen two things so fancy and pretty. We looked them up and down. Except for one being taller and the dresses different colors, they looked like identical fairy princesses. Dark brown shiny curls surrounded faces having not a freckle or spot. Their eyes were big and brown, as pretty as our favorite cow's. Their dresses were velvet, pleated and buttoned all down the front, with collars of white lace. Even though it was summer, they wore long stockings and black patent leather shoes.

They didn't seem to be bothered by our staring. The shortest one smiled at me—just to me (I'm sure).

Mom yelled about then, from the kitchen steps, "Agnes . . . you kids remember you got company.

Mind your manners . . . and don't git those girls all messed up!"

That sort of straightened us out. The girl that liked me asked, "Do you have horses? Madeline and I take riding lessons."

"No, we just have cows, goats, and chickens," Agnes said. They seemed a little disappointed but still followed us into the barn.

It wasn't long, though, before they were having a high old time. I showed Caroline how to jump down from the barn loft and land safely in a pile of hay. She was scared until she got the hang of it, then we could hardly get her away from the barn.

We went down into the pasture to catch frogs. They were all in hiding but Charley caught a big black snake that almost scared the tar out of Madeline. Before Charley turned it loose, both girls had worked up enough nerve to feel its smooth skin.

Agnes said, "I know . . . let's make fingernail files." She was off running for the barn. When she met us by the railroad track, she had half a dozen big nails in her hand. Agnes put her ear down on a rail. "Yep, a train's comin'." We laid the nails on the steel rail and stood back and waited. Sure enough, here came a double-engine coal train, lickety-split.

It made nice flat files for us, but Madeline was standing too close to the tracks and almost got hit by a huge chunk of black coal that come tumbling off a coal car. "Coal falls off all the time on this curve," Charley explained. "We haul it to our coal shed." He went to get the old wagon.

"Can I pull the wagon?" begged Madeline. We said okay. Caroline helped her, and they acted like it was fun to bring in coal.

Then we ran down to the roadway cut and slid down the dirt slopes. We knew they couldn't get hurt down there, because there were mounds of

69

loose dirt at the bottom of the slopes where Charley and I had been sliding down all summer.

Just when the Sneedham girls learned how to slide without falling, Mom was yelling from the house.

"Agnes . . . Charles! You bring them girls here right away. Time to go—Agnes . . . Charles!"

When we came around the corner of the house, Mom and Marie were standing by the car, not looking our direction.

"Wal, Marie . . . jobs are hard to get—even maid jobs. You better hang onto it, even if that man is a pest." Then they heard us and turned.

Mom's mouth flew open at the sight of the Sneedham girls. "Wal . . . wal, if that don't beat the dickens! Look at them clothes, all covered with dirt and hay. I'm goin' to take a stick to them kids of mine!"

Marie looked for a second like she was going to agree with Mom, but she just sighed and said, "No, Pearline. I got time to clean 'em up and change their clothes back at the hotel before we go get Mr. Sneedham. Bye, Hon. Bye, kids!" And Marie got into the big automobile.

Caroline and Madeline had to be told to get into the automobile. We sure hated to see them go. Caroline rolled down the window and smiled at me. "Goodbye, Edgar," she said. "I had a very nice time." Her hair was as wild as my sister's and her face was streaked with dirt, but she was still the prettiest girl I'd ever seen—and that was true for years.

———————

My brother Chuck and I are driving south from Carbondale, to kill a little time but also to take another look at the hill country. We are remembering some things about Dad—especially how he was such a take-charge guy. "Do you remember the rabid dog at the Nolte Place?" Chuck asks. "Sure . . . I remember almost everything," I reply. "Oh? . . . Do you remember when the African missionaries came to Mt. Joy—all the animal skins and drums they brought?" I have to admit that I do not remember the missionaries (how could I forget something that colorful? Maybe I was home sick).

We leave the main highway and drive on a blacktopped side road. We cross several lonesome country roads that look inviting and would be followed—if we had more time. Scores and scores of eastern blue jays are flitting through the underbrush and winging across the roadway. Chuck says the flocks are probably moving into the hills to eat cedar berries. It would be interesting to scout that out today.

We intersect a concrete road and find ourselves at a rock bluff that offers a panorama that I declare is about as subtly beautiful as any I have seen in the United States (I remind Chuck that I have worked or traveled in all the states). He nods agreement but points out that the last storm has taken the yellow leaves from the woods that blanket the miles and miles of terrain lying before us. "All you have left is basically the red," he says. "You should have seen it two weeks ago."

We drive into the ridgetop town of Alto Pass. I

71

comment: "If this place were in California, it would be a haven for tourists and artists." Chuck agrees. "Yeah," he adds, "those Californians would ruin it alright. Let's stop and ask how to get up to Bald Knob." I fuss a little about stretching our time this much, but am also eager to look—one more time—all the way into Missouri.

We come around the curve and leave the woods. There is the highest hill in Little Egypt and we feel lucky, because no one else is here. We walk around taking in the views that have resulted from millions of years of struggle between the Shawnee Hills (as they've attempted to rise and become mountains) and the big rivers, the Mississippi and the Ohio (as they've tried to cut them down and haul them away). I am thinking it would be a great day to drive all the way along the uplift to savor the rocky hills and wooded canyons.

Out of the blue, Chuck reflects, "A problem with being a success is—do you have time left to contemplate?—to enjoy things like this?" I ask, "You mean, did Dad have time?" Chuck doesn't answer. We get in the car to hurry back to Murphysboro, where we shall put on dark suits and sit in a solemn crowd.

For today is the day of Dad's funeral. "How fitting," Chuck and I discuss on the drive back, "that we think of this still as Dad's funeral—not a funeral **for** Dad."

Mad Dog

I sat up in bed and saw that Charley was already standing at a window looking out in the early morning light. "What was that terrible sound?" I asked. Before Charley could answer, it came again: a long blood-curdling howl that sent a shiver down my spine. "That's on our front porch!" Charley said as he ran from the bedroom. I followed him into the living room and found Mom, Dad, and Agnes looking out the front window.

Mom turned around and grabbed hold of Charley and then of me. "Listen here, kids. There's a mad dog on the front porch and under no circumstances are you kids to leave this house! Understand?" She didn't have to lay down the law to me; I wouldn't have left the house for anything. "Now you kids get dressed and just stay put in the kitchen until we figure out what to do."

Charley and I did just that but not until we had risked a peek out the front window. Milling around on the porch, head down—as if searching for something to bite—was the black and white collie that Charlie and I had seen yesterday. The dog had been running stiff-legged along the edge of the wheat field. And for some unknown reason, we had gone out of our way in avoiding him. Good thing!

As we dressed we heard Agnes asking Dad, "What are you going to do—shoot him?" Dad replied that he would, because no animal, or person even, survived being bitten by a mad dog. Mom added that her great uncle had died a horrible death, begging people to shoot him or give him a gun—from his cellar prison. Right after she said that, Mom yelled, "Oh, my goodness! Peggy's in the basement and I hope you boys closed that door!" There was the sound of Mom running into the kitchen.

Charley and I kind of sneaked into the kitchen, because neither of us could remember closing the cellar door last night. Sure enough, Mom's look told us that the cellar was open so that Peggy was free to just run out and the mad dog was free to come in. I felt awful but I was not about to venture outside the house. Even Charley looked like he wasn't going to risk being bitten by a slobbering mad dog.

Dad came in with a shotgun in his hands and settled who would do what. "Kids, your mom is going to close the cellar door. Agnes, you hold this door open so she can run back in if she has to. Edgar! Charles! You watch out the side windows and yell if you see the mad dog comin' around. I'd like to have Peggy shut up, in case I don't kill him on the first shot."

Just as I took my watch at the north windows, the mad dog went into another fit of howling and thrashing around on the front porch. I wondered if he could jump through a thin screen and an old glass window. The howling stopped and all was quiet on the front porch. I heard Mom opening the creaky back door (Boy, that's loud!) and Dad closing the breech of the shotgun.

For a while, those were the last intentional acts, for all hell broke loose. I heard a thump and Agnes yelled, "Mom's fell down the steps!" Charles yelled, "He's comin'! He's comin'!" Dad was yelling, "Back inside! Back inside!" I heard the cellar door slam shut and ran into the kitchen to see Dad pulling Mom into the house. She was holding her back and wincing with pain.

Dad sat Mom down and then went right out the back door, shotgun barrel pointed ahead and down. Very shortly we heard a shot and then another.

It wasn't over. That mad dog caused all kinds of trouble. Mom went to bed with her back. Dad took a pitchfork and carried the dead dog down to a pile of orchard prunings and burned him. Agnes spent all morning throwing pails of hot lye water on the steps and porches. Charley and I were sent into the barn and pasture to look over the animals for any fresh scars or signs of blood. About midmorning Peggy started barking, but we didn't let her out until noon. We kids thought that was pretty smart of her to know enough to stay out of the way of a mad dog. But Dad cautioned, "You boys keep an eye on Peggy. We can't be positive for about a month."

It seemed like a long, long time before we could again trust the animals.

We are on one of those red-eye flights that depart San Francisco late in the evening and arrive in Dulles Airport at dawn. We haven't yet crossed Nevada and the stranger beside me is already beginning to tell me what's bugging him about life—telling me more than he tells his boss, or perhaps his wife.

Without exchanging names, and knowing we shall not meet again, we talk into the night across Utah and Colorado . . . in this simulated friendship, far from home.

Summer Night

On summer Sunday nights on Grandpa's lawn out in the country, we three boys, Charley, Cousin David, and I, would lie on our backs and speak great truths and tell secrets while watching the sky for falling stars.

"There goes one!" we would shout, as a ball of fire tailed out from the Milky Way and plunged across the sky. The sudden change in the tone of our conversation would hush the katydids in the oak tree, so that we could hear the grown-ups visiting in the house behind us.

"Did you hear that?" David asked. "Mom is saying she hopes I do better in school this fall! Do you guys like school?"

"Yeah," I said.

"Why?"

"I like it because, if you do your work, you get to read all the encyclopedias, and you can find out about everything."

"Like what?"

"Like places where you want to go when you grow up . . . the Indians that used to live right here in these hills . . . the Shawnees . . . lots of things."

"When I grow up," said David, "I'm not going to be a farmer like my dad. Maybe I'll be an engineer like *your* dad."

"Dad used to be a farmer," said Charley, "and a miner, too. He's just now becoming an engineer by studyin' at night."

"What are you going to be, Charley?"

"I'm goin' to be a bum . . . like Uncle Ed."

"When I grow up, I'm not goin' to have kids," confided David.

"Why?"

"Cause they get sick and die, or they grow up and hang themselves."

"Aw, Wylie was the only one that did that," said Charley.

"Boy! Look at that. An orange star. Wow!"

"The encyclopedia says there are millions of stars."

"Heaven must be awfully big . . . God must be real rich."

"God doesn't spend money!"

"Then why do they take collections at church?" asked Charley.

"Would you like to be rich?" asked David.

"Yeah," I said, "if I was rich I would buy Agnes a new dress . . . and I would get Charley a bicycle."

"There goes one! Boy, look at that. Like the Fourth of July at Riverside Park!"

Then Mom would have to yell, "Edgar . . . Charley! Time to go. Say goodbye to David."

Even after a generation of children, [the] woods were still dangerous. Mrs. Imhoff's half sister was killed in the woods by a panther only eighty years ago.
—Imhoff family notes, Jackson County Historical Society, 1956

The Art of Being Brave

Bravery was very much on our minds when Charley and I were growing up in Little Egypt. We were told repeatedly that we came from brave ancestors. I knew that girls could be brave—because our sister Agnes was brave, and we had been taught about Joan of Arc. But bravery was not required of girls. Charley and I never doubted for an instant that boys could not become men until they had proven themselves by courageous acts—like those performed by Joshua, General Logan, Charles Lindberg, or Tom Mix.

I knew that Charley was brave because he could keep swinging his fists even when he was losing a fight to a bigger kid. But Charley said that he wasn't sure that he was brave enough. Charley was too polite to discuss my own condition, but I knew that I had never, ever, been brave.

A brave act was something you did with your eyes wide open, knowing for sure what could happen to you, but doing it anyway. Charley and I began testing ourselves by sliding down straw stacks, jumping from hay lofts, and teasing water moccasins. But soon, we came to admit, those were only games — not true tests of bravery. No. In our part of Jackson County there were only two real tests of bravery: playing escape on the railroad trestle and diving into the deep and dangerous waters of the abandoned brickyard pit. And some older boys had done both.

Charley and I decided to start with the railroad trestle where Billy Kent had passed the test. When Billy heard the whistle of an approaching train, he had taken a position between the rails of the Missouri and Pacific line, where that railroad crosses the Gulf Mobile and Ohio on a high trestle. There he had waited, as cool as a cucumber, until a train came into sight from around a sharp curve. Running in front of the train, Billy had crossed the trestle and had leaped safely from the path of the train before it could grind him into sausage.

There was no doubt that Billy had a lot of guts, but . . . maybe it had been a slow train? Charley and I figured that when you first glimpsed the big black engine, you had a little while to decide whether or not the train was coming too fast. If you guessed wrong, you might still be able to escape by falling down between the ties of the trestle and hanging on for dear life. But, it would look pretty chicken, and you would probably break your neck if you let go and fell below to the ground. On and on we talked and worried and practiced.

One Saturday, when Mom and Dad were away and Agnes was in the house reading, Charley and I went to the high trestle. I promised to race the second train if he would run before the first. We heard a train whistle blowing way over by Harrison. Good. It was heading the right direction.

When the train came into view, I was relieved to see that it was not going too fast. Anyway, Charlie took off, running between the tracks and well ahead of the train. It was going to be easy to be brave.

But a little brown and white dog ran quickly up the embankment, jumped between the rails, and followed Charley along the trestle. "Peggy! Peggy!" I screamed.

Charlie had almost cleared the trestle when he heard me and looked back over his shoulder to see Peggy losing ground to the oncoming train. He did not hesitate but ran back and caught up Peggy and—just before the train thundered between us blocking my view—he seemed to jump to the side of the tracks. The engineer was blowing the whistle wildly, and I feared for the worst while wanting to believe that I really had seen him escape.

In the terrible stillness that followed the passing of the train, Charley got up from the little space he had hunkered in—a little extra width of the trestle at center span—and came carrying Peggy safely from the trestle. Once on the embankment, he gave her to me and went over in the weeds and threw up. Charley came back looking very pale and said, "Let's not do that again. And that goes for the brick-yard pit, too!"

Today I catch a glimpse,
of not being in this place . . .
of not being.

No patterns of leaf green against oak gray
No red, white, and blue flag pulling in the wind,
No sun on my face.

I shall not care, too much.

There will be other trees,
So these must die.
There will be other symbols for other patriots,
who will someday unmast this one.
There will be another person standing here,
pondering in the sun.

Bring forth the new life!
Having been . . .
We shall not mind the not-being.

This Side of the River

"Overly warm for this time of year, ain't it?" Dad
said, acknowledging the folks waiting outside Mt.
Joy Lutheran Church. We had arrived just in time to
file in and take our places for evening service. I
understood soon why everyone was standing outside: the church was hot as an oven. The grown-ups
grabbed the cardboard fans that had been stuck in
the hymm books and began to beat away at the
humid, still air. On one side of the fan that I got

there was a big picture of Christ on the cross, on the other side a picture of him ascending to heaven. Whichever way you turned the fan, the eyes seemed to follow you.

On the trip from the Nolte Place, I had been wondering why Dad kept driving back to this old church instead of taking us to the new brick church in Murphysboro. Maybe it was because Reverend Boatman preached differently here. He didn't wear that black robe we had seen him wear in town. And in Mt. Joy he stood much closer to the congregation. Close enough to look us right in the eyes.

From the minute he started preaching tonight, he seemed to be looking right at me.

"God knows your every sin! . . . Do you?"

"You can't fool God! . . . Are you fooling yourself?"

Reverend Boatman talked about the guilt and uncleanliness of man, snared in the devil's trap.

I stopped fanning, for I was not going to have both Jesus and Boatman staring at me.

"We sang tonight, 'Now hear me while I pray: take all my sins away.' That's what we must do my sisters and brothers. We must come to the Lord as little children and beg forgiveness for our sins! . . . Now let us pray. Those who are able will kneel."

When I got down on my knees, I started thinking maybe I'd better confess. Anyway, God must already know that Charley and I have been talking about that eighth-grade girl's "you-know-whats" — the way they stuck out. I asked forgiveness for that but couldn't remember any other sins.

Boatman kept us in prayer for quite a while. I peeped across the aisle and saw Mr. Zimmerman rubbing his leg like he had a cramp and wondered if he was confessing a sin. I couldn't imagine what he, or his skinny old wife, could have done. Anytime we'd even passed their place, they'd been out working like mules. I watched Mrs. Zimmerman clasp and unclasp trembling hands. Her bonnet was pulled down tight on her head—even in this heat.

Then, we stood up and sang about how wonderful eternal life would be, after we quit this life of "grief and stress" and went "to rest beyond the river." Everyone pitched in and sang loud, like they were eager to go right now to that "place of rapture."

I knew that I was not ready to cross any river. And if that day ever came, I hoped that the last river I saw was prettier than the Big Muddy.

I could hardly wait for the benediction. Outside, the whippoorwills were calling, and, there would be time for Charley, David, and me to look for owls in the woods while the grownups hung around to talk about the weather and farming.

And tomorrow would be a good day to hunt for dewberries. The hot weather would be turning them purple and sweet.

For a time there, I was quite taken by the quick fixes of this age. "Got a problem? Simple: be positive, active, and—by all means—have faith, and the problem will be solved."

*Oh, yeah? Spend a day with **him**, and then you come back and tell me that the problem can be solved. You look me right in the eyes and you tell me that.*

Julius

Charley and I were out by the road to town, trying out our new cap guns by pretending to shoot birds. The bang of the cap guns frightened away the mockingbirds and the sparrows, but the clever old crows just moved higher in the wild cherry trees and went on feeding.

We were so busy scaring birds that we didn't notice him until he had come over the little hill on the road and was bearing down on us, in sort of a fast shuffle. We knew right away there was something wrong with him. I mean—different—in the way he sort of hung his head and grabbed the sides of his overalls as he walked along. He came up to us and stopped without really looking at us. We were relieved to see that he was grinning because he was head-and-shoulders taller than Charley.

"Hi," said Charley. "Did you walk out from town?" The big boy didn't answer. He just reached out a big hand and grabbed my cap gun. "See. Let see?" he said. Of course I let go of the cap gun, thinking that he just wanted to look at it. But, darned if he didn't hold it by his ear and shoot off the whole roll of caps as fast as he could pull the trigger: bang, bang, bang—until they were all gone.

By then Charley had gotten his dander up. He went over and grabbed away the gun and yelled at the big boy.

"You shot up all of Edgar's caps! You hog! They cost ten cents . . . a whole dime. You hog! You big hog!"

I thought Charley's temper had done it this time and got ready to run. But the big boy did a strange thing: he lowered his head and kind of hugged himself. Then he began shaking and crying and dropped down on the road.

Charley quickly got over being mad and stood

over him asking, "What's wrong? We didn't hurt you. What's wrong?" The big boy kept crying right there in the middle of the road. Charley and I exchanged scared looks. Oh boy! What if a car came flying over that hill? Did we cause this? Oh boy!

I went over to him and asked and asked his name. He finally muttered it. "His name is Julius," I yelled to Charley. Charley was glancing up and down the road. "We got to git him off to the side. What a mess! Let me try something."

Charley ran to the side of the road and held his cap gun high. "Julius," he called. "Julius, . . . if you come over here, I'll let you shoot up all my caps . . . Julius."

Julius rubbed his eyes and looked toward Charley, but still sat in the middle of the road. Oh my Lord! We heard a car coming! I ran over to Julius and caught him by the arm and tugged toward the side of the road. "Julius, if you go over there to Charley, you can be our friend, and you can come out and visit us again!"

And darned if he didn't get up and move (not fast enough for us) to the side of the road and stood there shooting all of Charley's last caps while the mailman whizzed by in his Model A.

Later, after we walked Julius to the top of the hill and headed him toward town, we sat on the road-bank and thought about the whole thing.

"Do you think he'll ever come back?" I asked Charley.

"Probly not . . . I hope not."

"I wouldn't mind. He was sort of fun."

"I guess so," admitted Charley. "At least he wasn't mean."

"How do you spose he got that way? Did he git hurt?"

"I dunno . . . I'm just glad it's not me."

Wracked with cancer pains that I could never endure, Doreen smiles and takes our hands and says, "I'm so happy to see you! I love you guys." Then I remember skinny little school kids that stood up under pain—stood up against all of us, for all of us. How remarkable a quality of the spirit—this thing we call courage.

In Unison

We are careful to avoid stepping on the big cups of the overcup oak tree as we walk through the wooded swamp on our way to school. I remember that when we lived in the shack we would gather the cups and play that they were furniture and wagons. In harvesting the acorns, squirrels have scattered the cups all along the shortcut we take now because it is fall and dry even in the bottomlands.

When we emerge from the woods, I inspect my new shoes and am glad to see there is not a spot of mud on them. Today, I want to look just as good as all the other kids. Most of them will be wearing new shoes and new clothes. This first week of school (until the first wash day), the schoolhouse will smell of new overalls and starched dresses and (until the first long rain) of new leather. Charley and I hurry across the newly mown schoolyard and enter the white frame building.

Most of the kids from last year were there, and I saw two new kids—about my age. I was happy to find that our old seats had been saved for us. We sat down and joined in the whispers and snickers of getting reacquainted, while being sure to watch the teacher for the call to attention. Through the big side windows of the school I saw the men out in the field cutting the last of the clover. I was pleased to be rid of the summer of work and seated safely in this place of books, thoughts, and smells of new things.

"Good morning," the teacher said with a smile. "Let's take attendance. When I call your name, please rise and remain standing." As he called our names, he recognized each of us, especially, with a little comment or smile. He repeated the names of the new kids: "Jane Baker and Harold Baker . . . we welcome you."

We had done the next part hundreds of times, but the teacher reminded us anyway: "Face the flag and place your right hand over your heart while we pledge allegiance to the flag of the United States." In unison we began, "I pledge allegiance to the flag of the United States of America and to the . . . "

"Hold it students," the teacher interrupted. "Harold, Jane . . . you must remain standing for the Pledge of Allegiance. Now, let's try it again."

We started again, but he stopped us even sooner, his voice rising like Dad's after he saw how Charley and I had painted the barn. "Do you hear me? Do you hear me!" He was standing right by their desks, looking down at them. "I said to stand and face the flag!"

I couldn't believe this was happening and wanted to be somewhere else—maybe even out in the hay fields. The new kids just sat there and wouldn't stand up. Their faces were red. The boy was looking down at his desk and beginning to cry. But the girl was staring right back at the teacher, her lips quivering. Finally, the teacher sighed, put his hands on his hips, and sent us out for recess—except for the Baker kids, whom he told to come up to his desk.

Out in the schoolyard, it was too soon to need the outhouse and we weren't yet warmed up to games. Besides, we wanted to know what was happening inside the schoolhouse. We wandered a respectful distance away and sat down where we could look into the schoolhouse. The teacher was standing up and shaking his finger right in the new kids' faces. We heard him say, "You will obey me or you will not come to this school!"

We could not hear the reply from the new kids, but it looked like they were crying, and I thought that I saw the girl shaking her head no. Then we saw the teacher sit down and write something on a sheet of paper and hand it to the girl. He motioned for them to leave the room.

After the recess bell, we returned to our desks, curious about the two empty seats but carefully silent around a teacher who acted mad the rest of the day.

At noon hour, I told Charley that I wished we had not brought these sandwiches but had gone home for lunch. I wanted to talk to Mom. After school, she listened calmly to our excited stories. "Those kids must have been doin' what their folks told 'em to do. Sounds like some kind of religion to me. You kids don't worry. It'll work out." Mom was usually right.

Next morning even slowpoke Charley was early as we arrived and waited to see if the new kids would show up and what would happen. And here they came walking right up to the teacher's desk and handing him a note! He read it, put it away neatly in his coat pocket, and—without saying a word—sat down at his desk and wrote another note. He gave the note to the girl and again motioned her toward the door. She was crying when she and her brother went out the door.

We thought, "Well, that's the end of that," but at recess a car drove down the lane to school. A man and a woman got out, each leading one of the new kids by the hand. They went into the schoolhouse and again we students gathered on the hillside to look into Number 5 Schoolhouse.

This time, the new kids' dad was pointing a finger at the teacher, and he was shouting "Read your Bible! The first commandment is: I am the Lord thy God; Thou shalt have no other gods before me. We pledge allegiance only to God—not to craven images! My children will obey you but not if you are disobeying God!" Then the whole family walked right out of the school, got in the car, and drove away.

The rest of the day the teacher was quiet and acted real bothered. He drove into town and back during the noon hour. At the end of the day, he announced there would be no school until Monday, because there was to be a special meeting of the school board.

I almost hated to go to school the next Monday. When Charley and I came out of the woods, we saw the new kids sitting solemnly on the glider that the WPA had installed for us to play on. I felt pity for those kids but went on inside without speaking.

The teacher was calm, just like he had been at the beginning of school. We stood up and pledged allegiance. After we had finished, the new kids came in and quietly took their seats.

The teacher explained that because the Bakers lived farther away than other students they would be allowed five extra minutes to take their seats after the schoolbell had rung—before they would be counted absent or tardy.

Thereafter, every school morning, rain or shine, the Bakers would not come into class until after we had pledged allegiance to the flag. Mom explained why that was all right, but we kids always treated them as different after that, which didn't make their lives any easier.

———————

Lights and lives
a million fold
glide by the window
of the DC-10
and disappear
like bubbles
in champagne.

Alone in the night
far from home
where home was . . .
"On the right side
of the aircraft
you can see
the lights of St. Louis."

Alone in the mind
far from home,
where home was . . .
when home was
a place to be left,
before home had value,
before home was sweet.

Storm A'comin'

When black clouds swept in from the west and the wind began to lay down the wheat in the field across the road, Mom would yell to gather her children and then hustle them down into the basement of the Nolte Place. There in the dark, amid the smell of stored potatoes and the sound of Peggy's growling, we would wait out the storm—half expecting to see the house lifted from over our heads or to emerge to find the barn and the cat blown to kingdom come.

However severe the storm, we felt safe in the deep basement and lucky to be escaping events and tragedies like those our folks had described many times in recalling the great tornado of 1925. As the rain and hail battered the Nolte House, we kids would tempt fate by asking Mom, again, to tell us about: the two dreadful lead funnels, like huge, black fangs, and the line of little devil twisters behind them . . . houses exploding in the air . . . the terrible roar and the smell of sulfur . . . how you could read the newspaper miles away by the light of the flames, as Murphysboro burned all that night . . . hail as big as hen eggs, settling to the ground as softly as snowflakes . . . the hundreds of dead and injured in makeshift morgues and hospitals.

Too soon the storm would pass over us, and we would have to open the inclined door and step out into cleaned air, to wet hens fussing in the yard and broken appletree limbs.

When we moved into town, we never quite adapted to living in a house that had no basement. "Foolish . . . foolish!" Mom would say as we huddled insecurely in the kitchen. And we would agree with her roundly, for we now had our own hard evidence. Hadn't Mr. Swanson, our next-door neighbor, lost a leg to the tornado? And each time we walked to school we passed the battered and crumbling foundations of homes blown away or burned down in March 1925. "Foolish, indeed," not to have a place to go in time of trouble.

Amateur genealogists admire the talent of Alex Haley but envy his luck. Imagine finding an old man who could recite the oral history of your family! Most of us who search for our roots spend weeks . . . months plodding through obscure and dull records compiled by church and state; almost every birth, wedding, death, arrest, transaction, military record, baptism, and confirmation has been recorded somewhere.

Thanks to the clerks and string savers, here and there are little pieces that can be put together to reveal the wanderings of our families and to help us discover who we are. For each of us is the product of the journeys of our ancestors—of the ships sailed, the wagons loaded, and the trails followed.

That is so in my family. My mother's people, the Cagles, differ from my father's people, the Imhoffs. When we were kids, we could not run or play, on the Sabbath day, in the presence of Grandpa Imhoff—and better to be seen than heard. But at Grandma Cagle's, Sunday was just another day to have fun, and children were even pestered to talk. There were other major differences in these families that shared a common origin in a Swiss-German valley and had migrated to Pennsylvania in the same wave of Protestants fleeing Europe.

I believe that the difference in the families began to form before the American Revolution when Leonard Cagle said goodbye to his Dutch neighbors—which included Imhoffs—and joined a wagon train of Scotch-Irish pioneers heading south down the long valleys of the Appalachian Mountains. They stopped and broke some land in Virginia. Leonard's sons drifted on to North Carolina and probably ruined some more land there, but this time penetrating farther into the western mountains. Their sons crossed the Great Smokies and settled in the mountains of Tennessee. Four generations and a hundred years after the family exodus from Pennsylvania, Tim Cagle launched a flatboat on the Cumberland River and floated north to southern Illinois, settling along Crab Orchard Creek "amid the wolves and rattlers," according to an old record I found.

While Tim Cagle was killing the rattlers ("three hundred in one year") and clearing the land, my father's great-grandfather, Andrew Imhoff, was moving his family from Pennsylvania in a Conestoga wagon, bringing along to Illinois the best of woodworking and blacksmithing tools and a persistent Swiss-German culture that had changed only grudgingly in the New World.

Not so with the Cagles, who during their separate journey had become a very different people. Since leaving Pennsylvania, the Cagles had acquired Irish eyes and humor, Cherokee cheek bones, southern warmth, and a hillbilly independence. They had become an easy people.

The Easy People

We kids were very proud of Dad's new shiny
Ford, and we were especially happy to wake up to a
rainfree Thanksgiving Day and know that the car
would look just as shiny when we drove in to
Grandma Cagle's place. Boy! Would they gather
round to admire this new car. I wished that Dad
would speed up and get there before the older boys
and the men went off on the big Thanksgiving Day
rabbit hunt.

But Dad had slowed down so much in the fog of
the Crab Orchard Bottoms that we drove up to the
Cagle's place too late to show off. From the sound of
shotguns coming from the weed fields, we knew
that the Cagles were already flushing out rabbits
and quail. My aunts—Liza, Mary, Marie, and Violet—came out and gave us a big welcome, smacking
kisses all over us kids. "You're gittin' so big, sweetie
pies!" Aunt Violet said. "Now you kids come in and
tell us all about school while we finish the breakfast
dishes."

We stepped inside to a rush of smells of baked
apples and pumpkin and got hugged again by
Grandma Cagle, who acted like she hadn't seen us
for years. After we told our stories, Agnes and I
found Grandma's stash of romance and detective
magazines and settled down by the pot-bellied
stove—we thought—to read away the morning
(Charley was outside looking for squirrels in the oak
trees that crowded the house). But there were too
many relatives running in and out for that to last.

Our cousins arrived from St. Louis, and Charley
and I joined them in feeding the pigs. Cousin Art
teased a pet squirrel—offering it corn, then jerking
away his hand—until it bit him. The excitement that
caused was forgotten when the men came trooping

in with dead rabbits and quail hanging all over them. The best shot, Uncle Wally must have killed a dozen rabbits. It was going to be a fantastic dinner.

During the skinning of the game, Wally offered each boy a chance to shoot his shotgun. Before they got down to me, Grandma Cagle came out of the house and gave the hunters the dickens, "You men are jist delighten' to see them boys get knocked ass-over-a-teakettle. You stop it rat now—and I don't mean mousey rat either!"

I was beginning to get sick of all the skinning and butchering. I went back into the house where two games of pinochle were already underway, amid much hollering and laughing. Grandma even let me hold a hand and play a couple of rounds. She would not quit playing, however, until she and Aunt Mary had beaten the men—even while people were yelling that the fried rabbit was going to get cold if the players didn't stop and set the tables.

After dinner, Uncle Rex brought out a guitar and played country songs while we sang along. Some of the men opened up another card game and some of the women gathered in the kitchen to gossip about ailments, folks running around, and the like. We kids sort of floated around from one exciting place to another, on the eve of that last big Thanksgiving Day gathering of the Cagles—before the older boys went to war.

———————

The homeless people hang out near the public buildings in Washington, D.C. If you look care-fully behind, in, and under the grand architecture and landscaping, you will see little nests of dirty clothes and boxes. Sometimes you will see the people themselves, but almost never will you com-municate with them. And, generally, they will avoid you: no more than a furtive glance from someone lying on a grate over a steam vent; a human sound coming from a pile of rags shrouded in the waste energy of the city.

This one startled me when he stepped in my path as I left the Old Executive Office Building. My first reaction was anger, especially when he got right in my face and nearly shouted: "Man, I'm hungry! I'm so hungry! Help me."

Then I actually looked into his eyes, saw him, and knew that he was telling the truth. I stood there feeling embarrassed, fumbling for all the small change I had on me—about four dollars—and handing it to him. He took the change without saying another word as I hurried away.

A Letter to Uncle Ed

In 1940, I wrote my first letter. It was a letter to my namesake, Uncle Ed. He was the only one in the family who ever went on the bum. I kept the letter a secret from Charley and everyone else—because they would have said I was being silly. I had a secret plan, too, for getting the letter to Uncle Ed, who was out west "God-knows-where," Dad said.

95

I curled the envelope and pushed it into a glass bottle that I hid under a loose board in the barn flooring. Bums always came by our barn, to or from the railroad tracks. When spring came, a lot of them would be traveling again. I figured that I would halt one of them, out behind the barn, and ask him to pass my letter along to Edgar Wallace, my namesake.

It might work! I would look at their faces until I found one I could trust. Of course, he would have to be heading out west.

I could just picture Uncle Ed getting up from a campfire, standing tall, and answering: "Yeah, I'm Ed Wallace. What's it to ya?" The other bum would quickly pull an old soiled letter from his tow sack and say, "No offense . . . letter for ya . . . no offense." I could just see Uncle Ed relax and sit down to read my letter by the campfire, grinning while the coyotes howled and the wind blew down from the mountains.

Dear Uncle Ed,
I am your namesake. My name is Edgar Imhoff.
If this letter finds you I hope you are well and have gotten over the TB. Mom said you left before I was born and don't know you have a nephuw named after you. Mom and Grandma talk about you a lot and wish you could come home. I feel like I knowed you a long time. Aunt Liza told me you were not afraid of the devil. I want you to come and tell me about all the things you saw because I want to go there to. Love.
P.S. We have a lot of food at this place. Mom feeds men all the time. Come to Murphysboro and go north to #5 School. We live just this side.

We moved, that summer, before I ever found anyone to carry my special letter. It's probably still there under the old barn floor, never seen again, never found—like my Uncle Ed.

Like the little gray clouds that skirt before a strong squall line, there are messengers of change, too, in human affairs that signal that something important is sweeping relentlessly upon us. World War II came on that way, advancing to change our lives, even while some of us were denying its approach or contesting its right to rout us from our comfortable places and to separate us from the things we loved.

View from an Apple Tree

When Peggy and I returned from picking dewberries, Mom was in the kitchen listening to the radio. The regular program was interrupted for a special broadcast. In a troubled voice—through breaks in a weak transmission, the correspondent reported the fall of Paris.

I listened for a moment before saying, "Well . . . guess I'd better milk the goats." Mom threw me an annoyed "shssh!" and waved me out the door as she bent over the radio to catch the fading message coming from a place so far away and so different that I couldn't understand what on earth it had to do with us here on the Nolte Place.

A few weeks later, Dad came home early one day and went straight into the house—without waving at Charley and me, who were out worming the garden. Charley set down his can of kerosene and went in to find out what was happening. When he returned, he just walked on by me without saying anything and climbed into an apple tree. I knew it was serious, so I ran down to ask what Dad had said to Mom.

"We're moving," Charley said.

"No we're not! Why would we do a thing like that?"

"Yep, and we're going to get rid of all the animals."

"You're lying! You're makin' this up, Charley!"

"No use bawling about it. We're movin' to town."

"Why?"

"Because Dad has a new job building a defense plant over at Crab Orchard, and he won't be home much to look after things."

"Yeah . . . but we do that now!"

"Dad says he doesn't want Mom to stay out here alone by the railroad track, and besides—he thinks the schools are better in town and we'd be able to see more kids our age."

I remember not being able to listen any more and then running away to join the cows in the pasture. They didn't ask me to stop crying.

Despite all our pleas and tears—from Agnes and me anyway (Charley wouldn't cry)—we began to lose the Nolte Place that beautiful summer of 1940. When they came to get the cows, I hid up in an apple tree as Old Bird, bawling in protest, was loaded into a truck. Who wouldn't bawl to leave our green pasture with its own spring of sweet water and its shade of walnut trees.

I managed to be out berry picking when the last goat was taken; but I really didn't care that much when they came for the messy rabbits and the chickens.

At least we still had Peggy, the dog, and Ole Puss, the cat. Then, at breakfast, about a week before we were to move, Mom said, right out of the blue: "Edgar, you know we can't take Ole Puss to town."

I covered my ears and shook my head "No" until Mom pulled my arm away and said: "Now listen! If you think this is easy for me, you got another think comin'. Honey, cats are tied to a place. She belongs on *this* place! The next people will take care of her."

But I never accepted that logic. How on earth, I thought, could we leave behind an animal that loved us so much. Why even when she didn't have kittens she would hunt and bring us rabbits, quail, and even big snakes and lay them at the back door, as if to say, "I'm doing my part to help this family."

From a seat in my favorite apple tree, I looked across the fields and buildings of our place and still could not believe that we were leaving, and leaving Ole Puss behind. I had been dreaming about her—horrible dreams in which, as we loaded the last of our stuff and got into the truck, Ole Puss comes walking softpawed out of the weed field. She is so surprised to see what we are doing that she drops her mouse and meows: "What's this? You're leaving? . . . You didn't tell me?" And then as Dad guns the engine to get away, she cries out after us, "Traitor! . . . traitor! . . . traitor!"

As the actual day drew closer, I could hardly bear to pet Ole Puss, but I kept close track of her comings and goings and came to know many of her secrets by following her trails. On the day itself, I was greatly relieved when we pulled away with the last load while she was still out hunting. I sat in the back of the truck to Murphysboro hugging Peggy and seeing Ole Puss in my mind. Just about now, I knew she would be watching the young squirrels frolicking down in the hickory woods.

Town

A downtown view of pre-World War II Murphysboro. Courtesy of Jackson County Historical Society, Murphysboro, Illinois.

In a Harris tweed jacket, at dawn, I walk down Main Street and see the local men in John Deere caps and Dekalb caps firing up their trucks for a day of hauling hogs and grain. I buy a paper but throw it away within two blocks, because it is full of stories about people I don't know and places I have forgotten.

Returning to Main Street, I discover that several trucks are parked at an eating place announced as Hilda's Pantry. I go inside and sit next to a John Deere and a Dekalb. They are eating eggs, sausage, and potatoes. I order a half a grapefruit (which Hilda doesn't have), then, Product 19 (which Hilda doesn't have). Hilda is beginning to act impatient. The John Deere quits talking hogs and stares at me. Some guys quit talking weed killers and look me over. I am beginning to get that "new-kid-in-town" feeling. I order quickly: "Just give me a big bowl of oatmeal and some black coffee . . . fine!"

The Welcome
(1941)

Why were we doing such a dumb thing as moving into this house on Herbert Street! It was not much more than a box that had been quartered into four rooms. There were houses on all sides so that people could look in at us, but we couldn't look out and see anything worthwhile—not an orchard, or a train, or the rain coming across the fields. Charley and I helped carry in our things, but I just knew that nothing good would come of this.

And, right away, some bad things did happen. To get to junior high school, we had to walk about a half-mile—crossing a railroad switchyard on the way. The first time I walked across the tracks (alone, for Charley was late), I got beat up—nose bloodied and glasses broken—by a gang of mean kids.

I arrived late to school, after wandering several blocks out of the way. When I finally found Logan Junior High School, and then the principal's office, they scolded me and taped together my glasses so I could attend classes. In my first room someone whispered loudly at me, "Hey, four eyes. We're going to git you good next time!" In the hallway, an eighth grader shoved me and said, "Stay out of the way, gogglehead!"

Charley could not help me. This was not country school, with all the students in one room. Charley was in other classes in a different part of the building, and he was having his own problems.

The next morning, like a scared rabbit, I walked a different route to school. In a few days, Bob, a boy who lived well away from our street, joined me in walking to school. At first I thought that he was a friend. One morning he showed me what he called a "hot book." It was a little cheap-looking cartoon book showing people doing things. I was embarrassed but I laughed. Bob got real excited talking about the cartoon characters. The next morning I tried to miss Bob by turning a block sooner than usual, but when I reached an open field, there he was waiting for me.

Bob was not very friendly this time and tried to twist my arm. I pretended that he was just playing and pulled loose. Thereafter, every morning he teased or attempted some type of torment—once pulling a knife on me.

Then, the worst thing in the world happened. One morning I woke up to find I had wet the bed. Mom was very nice about "the accident" and just changed the sheets without saying much. But when it happened on the next day I was heartsick, and I could see that Mom was getting worried. I had never done this before, not since I was a baby.

For several nights I kept wetting the bed. In disgust, Charley moved out of our room and slept in the kitchen. Dad gave me a severe talking-to, saying that he knew it was because I was "playing with myself." Mom shushed Dad off and was real sweet. I felt horrible.

On a Saturday, when I was sweeping leaves from the front porch, a towheaded boy on a bicycle rode up and said, "Hi. I'm Billy Boucher. What's your name?" He looked like a nice kid, but . . . I didn't know. Before long, though, I was doubled up behind him on my first bike ride. We rode over to a softball diamond where Billy showed me how to find pop bottles discarded at ball games. We found six bottles that we took to Whitson-Rigg's store and exchanged for candy.

In the afternoon, Billy came by again—wanting to know if I could come over to his place to read comic books. My mom looked him over and smiled and said, "Wal, Edgar . . . you can chop kindling later." There were a lot of other kids over at Billy's—boys from Herbert Street—and we had a great time.

The next morning I woke up in a dry bed. Monday morning the bed was again dry, and Charley said that he might move back in to our room.

On my way to school, I saw Bob waiting for me at the edge of the field. He had a small stick in his hand. As I came closer, he began to swat his pants leg with the stick and flinch and yell "ouch!" Then he would smile in my direction.

I knew what I was going to do. Bob made a move as if to hit me with the stick, but I drew back the brickbat I had been holding behind my back. "If you ever bother me again, I'm going to smash you in the face!" I said. That was about the last I saw of Bob and the beginning of a lot of fun on Herbert Street.

The last time I saw her was during the Korean War. I had overseas orders in my pocket and my leave time was running out. She looked the same as when she had taught in Logan Junior High: hair drawn back into a severe bun, exposing an intense face; body, stout—but not without grace. As we approached on the sidewalk, I contemplated speaking to her—wanting to hear again the rich voice, but she stopped to look into a store window. I walked by without a word. After several paces, however, I felt that I really needed to talk with her, and I turned back—only to find that she had disappeared into a shop. I waited for a while but walked away when I became too self-conscious of being a young soldier standing in uniform on the streets of Murphysboro in broad daylight, waiting for a seventh-grade school teacher.

A Neutral Zone

The student body of Logan Junior High met weekly in a general assembly—for announcements and ceremonies, but mainly to sing with Miss McMahon. In the fall of 1941, each student was issued a little purple-backed book of songs that celebrated virtue, home, and love. In a strong, clear alto, a joyous Miss McMahon would lead us through this song book, starting with her favorite number, which began:

> The bells of St. Mary's
> Ah hear they are calling,
> the young loves, the true loves,
> that come from the sea.

December came along and with it the attack on Pearl Harbor. In the new year, the school distributed new songs—about caissons rolling along, and passing the ammunition and going down in flames. It seemed that each of us had a relative fighting or training to fight. Singing the war songs almost made us feel like we were there with them. We became charged with a fervor that made us barely controllable.

Miss McMahon did not appreciate the rowdy way we sang the new songs, especially the boys, stamping their feet during marching songs and vying for each other's attention by making Nazi salutes and slant eyes to mock the enemies. Miss McMahon failed to get us to sing the war songs with a "nice enthusiasm," the same way we sang the old favorites. After a few assemblies, she was replaced permanently as a song leader, and we never again sang "The Bells of St. Mary's."

By the spring of 1942, World War II was consuming our interests and our energies. We kids carried out drives to collect scrap iron, tin cans, metal foil, and other materials useful in the making of bombs, bullets, and armament. These war-effort activities

intruded into the classroom. It was not unusual to
see kids knitting in the study hall—making
sweaters and mufflers for servicemen—or kids clustered in corners of the study hall or in classrooms
organizing war-related activities.

Competition was keen among the student volun-
teers. I remember hard feelings and squabbles over
prizes. John Ed beat me in the tinfoil contest by having his father save all the sweepings from the family
saloon, obviously a treasure trove of discarded cigarette packs containing precious tinfoil. I had not
scrounged along every sidewalk and roadside ditch
just to come in second; and I was telling John Ed
this all the way into Miss McMahon's classroom—
when a firm hand clamped on my arm and the suddenly authoritative voice of Miss McMahon started
giving us the devil.

> Class! Pay attention! Edgar, John, sit down! I
> wish that you could see yourselves as I see you.
> You would be shocked to discover how discour-
> teous and unruly you are becoming! No doubt
> it is this war.
>
> Now, in this classroom, no more talk of war.
> Let us agree that this is a neutral zone. Please
> leave your war efforts at the door, before you
> enter this room. Do we have an agreement? Do
> I have your word on it?

"Yes, ma'am, yes, ma'am," we mumbled. When
Miss McMahon got fired up, she was really
impressive.

We kept our agreement with Miss McMahon. Her
classroom remained neutral. In government class we
studied military rank and even elected a student
"company commander." And in science we learned
how gunpowder was made. But in language class
we just diagramed sentences and conjugated verbs.

It wasn't always a sacrifice, because if we performed well, Miss McMahon would read to us—and she read even better than she sang. The reading material was always about nature, love, and overcoming evil—usually in the Canadian wilderness. Before the school year ended, I believe she had read to us all of James Oliver Curwood's *Kazan*.

We began to look forward to Miss McMahon's readings. There was something very restful about arriving in her room, after shouting ourselves hoarse in the assembly hall or in the gym. She had switched the order of class activities so that now she read to us before we worked. She would pick up *Kazan* and away we would go with her to some other place.

> The rocks, the ridges and the valleys were taking on a warmer glow. The poplar trees were ready to burst. The scent of balsam and of spruce grew heavier in the air each day, and all through the wilderness, in plain and forest, there was the rippling murmur of the spring floods finding their way to Hudson Bay.

When Grandma Cagle was ninety-five, I got a long distance call, "Edgar, your Grandma will not last the winter." Thereupon, I made a special trip from the East Coast to Johnson City. I arrived at Aunt Marie's to find other relatives—summoned under the same general alarm. Hugging and hand-

shaking my way to the center of the room, I found poor old Grandma in a wheelchair; she looked tired and confused but recognized me. Despite the din around us, we were beginning to have a decent conversation. Then, Mom interrupted to say that Grandma had been looking forward to playing me a game of checkers (sure, Grandma, . . . for old times sake). As we set up the board, Grandma began to show a little spark. The crowd had moved off to find food and anything else more interesting than a game of checkers.

I began to play quickly and generously. Too late I realized that Grandma was playing by our old rules: "Have fun, but play to win." Down nine to six with a king gnawing at my backside, I raised my eyes from the board to see her sitting upright in the chair looking not a day over 75. Now, she was going to toy with me.

Staring at the disaster on the board, I could feel the relatives crowding back into the room, reassembling to see Edgar get his comeuppance (the word that I was getting beaten had spread fast).

Using every move I could remember—and with some luck—I finally played Grandma Cagle to a draw. Smiling and laughing, she asked, "Who taught you how to play, Edgar?" I replied so the whole crowd could hear, "You did, Grandma, in the house in the woods. You did."

The Queen of Checkers

My first awareness of the new day was that I was already hot and sticky. I remembered that Charley and I were staying at Grandma Cagle's place north of Marion and that it was Saturday. Charley was still sleeping. The day before, we had worked hard for

Grandma—cleaning the henhouse, tearing down an old shed, and hoeing the garden. She had just kept bragging on us all day, so . . . what else could we do?

A screech of fighting crows and jaybirds came from the oak trees. I heard the muffled sounds of Grandpa and Grandma talking, heatedly, and the sound of Grandpa's coal truck leaving the farm. Then, from right in the next room, I heard Grandma's voice, little more than a whisper. I couldn't make out the words, but it almost sounded like praying. I sat up in bed and cocked my head to the wall. "Oh Lord, (mumble . . . mumble)." Grandma was praying!

I became embarrassed and turned away but her voice became stronger and I could hear every word:

> And Lord, look after Charley and Edgar. They are good boys, helpin' out all they can on this little old farm . . . but times a comin' when the Devil will tempt their flesh. Protect them, Lord, . . . and Lord, if you will just tell Edgar to git out of bed and go feed the stock, I'll make him a handsome breakfast.

My feet hit the floor. Doggone it! Just like Grandma to pull something like that.

As we finished our bacon and eggs, Grandma told us her plans for the day:

> Boys, this is your first Saturday with your Grandma. One thing you'll learn about me: I like to have fun! As long as poor people haf to work all the time anyhow, they might jist as well have some fun. When I was fourteen, I married a coal miner . . . had eight kids . . . held my dyin' mother in these arms. There's nothin' can get you down unless you let it.
>
> Edgar, you go pick some beans and tomatoes

for Sunday company. Charley, you load the eggs in the pick-up. Soon's you're done, we're goin' to town to trade them eggs for show money . . . there's a double feature at the Orpheum!

At the motion picture house in Marion, Grandma gave the man our tickets and we entered the cool and jeweled interior. As we sank onto velvet seats, the light faded to a blackness that extinguished the glitter of the chandeliers and all thoughts of the common world.

Music blared and huge curtains rippled open to expose another world, and eagerly we entered it. In the Battle of Midway, I shot down zero fighters without flinching from the bullets that tore through my own plane. Within the purple shadows of the snowcapped Sierra, I rescued a golden-haired girl— pulling her upon my saddle as my horse galloped wildly by her and as I shot back over my shoulder to hold off the bad men. Although the golden girl loved me desperately, I rode off into the mountains with my cowboy pals while she waved sadly from the train station.

As if that were not enough for one day, I also danced with Ginger Rogers, cheered on by throngs—as I matched my lovely partner's unbeliev- able grace in floating down marble stairways and gliding across glass tabletops.

But the chandeliers did again brighten in the Orpheum Theater. And the curtains closed to cover the screen. We got up and slowly filed outside into an irritation of light and heat. Still lingering in the world beyond the screen, I looked out upon the Marion square and saw myself as an awkward, bespectacled boy about to climb into the back of an old pickup. Grandma said it for all three of us, as she fumbled to find her keys: "Lordy, sometimes wouldn't you jist love to be somebody else!"

I am one of many amateur researchers who frequent the dark interior of the National Archives Building, pouring over musty old documents and letters. I am interested especially in the American Civil War. You would be amazed to see the kind of detailed records our country keeps on war veterans and pensioners. Mostly the research is tedious and uninspiring. Once in a great while, though, I retrieve a record folder that holds surprises and secrets. That is the way it has been with the papers of Ananias and his brother Jim. And I would not have searched so thoroughly if I hadn't heard Grandpa say that summer, "When Ananias was your age . . . " and "Now . . . don't be an Uncle Jim!"

Ananias

During the summer that Charley and I worked for Grandpa as hired hands, I failed miserably at two tasks: unloading hay in the mow of the barn and breaking land with a moldboard plow. Grandpa forgave me the one sin—rationalizing that I had inherited the hay fever from Grandma—but he never let up on my inability to cut a straight deep furrow through a grassy meadow that he called the "bounty land" or, sometimes, "Uncle Ananias' land."

During one week, we tried several times: Grandpa showing me how to wrap the reins tight around the wide handles of the plow and how to throw my slight weight into guiding the blade so that the heavy soil was peeled back in neat rows.

But it never worked for me, no matter how hard I tried: the horses would stumble over my crooked rows and turn their heads to look at me wild-eyed, and Grandpa would walk alongside spitting tobacco juice with vehemence. One day he sent me to fetch the water jug from the creek; then lectured me while we sat in the shade.

"Edgar, if you're goin' to be a farmer, you got to be able to break your own land. Your Uncle Ananias broke land like this when he was your age . . . when he weren't much older, he went off to the Civil War . . . died a hero at Vicksburg. You remember! His enlistment money bought this land. Now, let's see if you can plow it like a man!"

And I would try it again.

Forty years later it is time to quit the search. Researching in the National Archives Building, I have finished reading the last record pertaining to Ananias Imhoff, Private, Co. D, 31st Illinois Infantry. Before returning the file folder to the librarian, I write my name and address on the registration form provided to enable researchers to communicate with each other. It is the only entry ever made on the folder, and the records have been available for a hundred years . . . I would really like to tell someone about this. "Ah, Grandpa. If we could just sit in the shade again, I would tell you about the Ananias that I found." He was a small man (boy?)—almost tiny. He was illiterate and could only enter an "X" on the signature block of his enlistment papers. Wondering about his size, I cross-checked his declaration of age (twenty) with the census records and discovered that he had lied, under oath, and was really only seventeen. Otherwise, Ananias seems to have behaved like a model son. He had the government pay the enlistment bounty to his mother, and he even sent her all his military pay, which must have made him quite a wet blanket in camps such as Cairo and Lake Providence, when other soldiers were indulging generously in purchased vices. There is no indication in the archives that Ananias—in contrast to Uncle Jim—did anything special to bring about the surrender of Vicksburg.

One night in late June of 1863—when the fall of the besieged city was imminent—the Confederate cavalrymen came upon Ananias on picket duty in the rear of Vicksburg and brushed him aside as easily as the killing of a fly. He is buried in an unknown grave somewhere in Mississippi—far from his mother in Mt. Joy Cemetery—far from the grassy meadow I could never break.

I also searched the files of the National Archives for records pertaining to the brother of Ananais, Private James Imhoff. Unlike his brother Ananias, Uncle Jim survived the Civil War and limped home to marry his childhood sweetheart. But, Jim never quite overcame the effects of multiple wounds and fevers. And there really wasn't much of a place for him back home in Illinois. His brothers—particularly his ambitious older brother, Henry—had prospered at farming while Jim and Ananias were at war. Henry had inherited the family farm, acquired Ananias' bounty land, and had rented more land. Henry was on his way to becoming one of Jackson County's "prominent agriculturists."

Uncle Jim

My grandfather was one of the several sons of Henry. Sometimes when Grandpa and I were driving the team to town, he would talk a little about his uncles—especially Jim.

> A little tighter on the reins, Edgar! You got to boss these horses. You'll never make a teamster like Uncle Jim. Now there's a feller that could drive a twelve-horse reaper . . . but didn't do him no good. He jist couldn't keep a job. No, you don't want to be like Uncle Jim. . . . Here give me the reins. I'll take 'em the rest of the way.

Sometimes I would ask Grandpa what happened to Uncle Jim. Grandpa provided little detail.

"Oh, Uncle Jim tried about everything: blacksmithing, teamstering, road work—even hired out to Henry, but he couldn't keep a job. He had a hard time raisin' a family. Jim finally went out west with one of his boys; died out there somewhere."

> *When the records of James Imhoff, Private, Co. D, 31st Illinois Infantry were delivered to me in the Archives Building, I was surprised at their volume. As I studied them, the life of the war veteran unfolded. Uncle Jim's last fight wasn't in General Sherman's Carolina campaign. No. His last fight was for a decent invalid pension.*
>
> *In 1868, Uncle Jim first declared for a pension, acknowledging more or less that he was not able to hold his own in the labor-intensive economy of the time. Despite numerous letters of evidence from comrades-in-arms attesting to his wounds, despite many affidavits from doctors describing his pathetic physical condition, and even in the face of letters of influence from politicians (one mentioned*

the votes that could be garnered by helping this veteran), Uncle Jim never received an adequate pension. His last letter to the Pension Bureau was written in December, 1926:

I am writing you for information as to what you have done in regards to my increase I applied for several months ago/Since sending in my doctors report as requested by you (I) have not heard from you/Now please inform me if it has been received or not/I am growing very feeble more and more every day. Have to have a person to stay with me all the time/It will not be long any more that the government will have to pay me and I would like very much to get it while I live as my son and wife have a hard struggle to care for me and pay my medicine bills and doctor bills/and when the last taps are sounded they will have to bear the burden. My pension certificate is No. 192739.

Uncle Jim's son had to care for the old bedridden soldier until his death in 1928. But, the government finally came through: Private James Imhoff, sharpshooter, was buried in a memorial cemetery set in the midst of some of the most valuable real estate in California. I have visited the site. Looking up from the modest headstone at his grave, one sees the high rises and mansions spilling over the hills of Hollywood.

"Yeah, we finally took care of that old soldier."

———————

Betty and I are thumbing through an old high school annual, looking for photographs of a few special people. "Let's see. Where is Elmus Norris? He was a class act. Hmm . . . no photo under the N's . . . why? . . . hmm. Betty, look at this! You are not going to believe this! Elmo and all the other black students are lumped together on the last page! And look at the poor quality of their photos compared to those of us white students. The photographer didn't even bother to change the shutter opening!"

Betty places it in perspective: "I know it's terrible," she says. "But don't you think that your outrage comes about forty years too late?"

The People down by the River

When I was four years old (I am told) and enjoying the rare privilege of riding in my uncle's coal truck, we saw children with dark skin playing near some shacks and patches of corn down near the Big Muddy River. "Why are they that color?" I asked. "Because they are dirty," replied my uncle. Later, laughing about the incident to my family, my uncle reported that I had thought for a moment and then asked, "Why don't they wash in the river?" My mother says that she scolded my uncle: "The Bible teaches you must love thy neighbor as thyself— whatever his color. Don't you be sayin' things like that to a child!"

Mom may have straightened out my uncle, but she couldn't have made a dent in the white society of southern Illinois in the 1930s and 1940s. Oh, it wasn't that certain parents, teachers, and preachers did not try, providing lessons "that we are all one race" — lectures about the rights of man. The prevailing lessons, however, were "understandings" that were just passing around and around: stories of laziness — chuckled about under shade trees on a Sunday afternoon; jokes told in blackface acts at medicine shows — of fears of ghosts and of sexual prowess; rhymes sung in schoolyards while skipping rope — "Eenie, meenie, minie, moe. . . . " Strange that we would talk so much about people that we seldom saw: no one I knew had any black neighbors; there were no blacks in grade school or in junior high, and none in my church; sometimes you would see them on the streets of Murphysboro, but you never knew their names. For most young whites, the first real encounter with the people down by the river was in high school.

As my education moved along, I came to believe that I could identify and judge the prejudices of my society. Nevertheless, I was surprised to find that the first black student to sit beside me in high school was very bright and that he had pimples — just like me.

———————————

Besides new leaves
spring brings
a deep longing
for lives
never lived—
for lands
never seen.

In the spring rains
we feel
our ancestors' tears,
in the winds
hear
their sighs
of regret.

Fires in the field
are set—
I believe—
to consume
last year's cares,
and free
this year's dreams.

Some day . . .
we will go.
Finally,
we will go—
to find the place
from whence
the spring winds blow.

Grandpa's West Wind

Every time we boys looked at Grandpa's horse, Old Bill, we could just see him in a western movie—blazed face, flowing mane, sleek body. And that's sort of where Grandpa got Old Bill; he had been caught in a roundup of wild horses and shipped east as a plow horse.

Grandpa and Old Bill got along pretty well, even though the horse was ornery. When I tried to hitch him up, Old Bill would pinch a welt on my back. But I felt sorry for the horse. Here he'd been roaming the range free and wild, making his own decisions about where to go, what to eat, where to sleep at night. Now his whole life added up to four words: *whoa*, *giddup*, *gee*, and *haw*. What a fate for a western bronco!

Sometimes I would sneak Old Bill an extra ear or two of corn and just sit and watch him toss his head. He still looked like a cowboy's horse, even with harness marks beginning to show on his coat. Grandpa noticed I was partial to Old Bill and scolded me, "Now, you don't want to go babyin' stock! The Lord put that animal on this earth for our purposes."

Most of the time, Old Bill agreed with Grandpa and worked faithfully like a regular plow horse—except in the spring. When warm winds blew in from the southwest, Old Bill "didn't behave normal," said Grandpa. The horse would race around the barnyard, nostrils flared and tail held high. If Grandpa wanted to start some field work, he had a devil of a time catchin' Old Bill—especially with Grandpa having a bad leg.

Grandpa would run around chasing that horse—trying to put a halter on him while getting madder and madder. Grandpa would finally give up and wait until Old Bill went into the barn for his evening grain—which put the work off until tomorrow.

One Saturday in spring, just before Grandpa sold his place and moved to town, Dad and I stopped by. "Where's Grandpa?" I asked Grandma. "He's down in the barnyard fussin' with Old Bill," she frowned. I left Dad laughing with Grandma.

Grandpa hadn't seen us drive up. He was sitting on the board fence, watching Old Bill prance around and snort. For some unknown reason (guess I was growing up), I didn't announce my arrival. That's how come I heard Grandpa say something to Old Bill that I have always remembered, but has been just between me and Grandpa and Old Bill. He said: "Go ahead and run around, you crazy fool! See what good it'll do you. If'n I was a young man agin, maybe I'd just saddle you up and we'd ride outta here, and just keep goin'. You'd like that, wouldn't you Bill?"

From the airport south of Knoxville, I see that the Great Smokies have not changed during the forty years that have passed. I have forgotten the way these mountains gather themselves into successive ridges that rise higher and higher but become increasingly obscure with distance.

The Secret Year

In 1943, Charley and I arrived in Knoxville on a Greyhound bus. I was 13; he had just turned 15. On an all-night ride across the length of Tennessee, we stood in the aisle most of the trip. The bus had been crowded from the start. Many soldiers and sailors were aboard with their wives or sweethearts, so we did not mind doing our share for the war effort while the couples snuggled and tried to sleep. Anyway, we were too excited to sleep. Our adventure had come as a complete surprise.

Late in the summer in which Charley and I were staying at Grandpa Imhoff's, we had received a short letter from Mom, who had left Murphysboro with Agnes to spend the summer with Dad out in Kansas, where he was building a war plant. The letter read:

> Enclosed is $20 and two bus tickets for you boys to travel from Carbondale to Knoxville. Have Uncle Clyde take you to Carbondale on the morning of September 3. Be at the bus station no later than 9 o'clock. Dad and I will meet you at the bus station in Knoxville on the next day. Bring all your clothes in that old suitcase we left you.
>
> Your Dad is going to help build a big war plant down in Tennessee. He says that you are *not* to go around telling people about this. If you don't understand this or there are any problems, you have somebody go into town and call us right away.
>
> Love—Mom, Dad, and Agnes

Our folks were there to meet us in Knoxville. We piled into the Ford, more anxious to see the new home than to sleep.

Now, in 1983, I drive a rental car north on Central Avenue, past old and close set houses, following an abandoned streetcar route marked by a difference in pavement where the tracks have been removed. Approaching a right-angle bend in the old streetcar route, I park and remain in the car looking at a low, worn building labeled "laundromat" by a faded sign. Looks like the place all right. I wonder if we were the last family to actually live in there?

It was not much to look at, either, that morning in 1943. Just a small one-room store building with frontal full-length glass windows that Mom had coated with Bon Ami to shut out prying eyes. As we stood speechless and stared, Dad reminded us, "There's a war on and a lot of other people have moved down here to work at Oak Ridge. We'll have to make do with this until something else opens up."

We were too tired to complain. Mom had hung old bed sheets to partition the building into sleeping areas. Charley and I went in and flopped down on a bed and fell asleep.

Not for long, though. I dreamed that I heard a train wreck, a horribly loud screech of iron on iron and the sound of a bell warning of the disaster. Charley and I jumped up and stumbled into the middle of the building where Mom and Dad were sitting at a makeshift table. "What was that noise?!" I asked. Mom said, "Go back to sleep, kids. That's just a streetcar. They come by here every half-hour and turn a sharp corner right outside this door. You'll git used to it."

Mom was right. We did get used to the streetcars. We even became accustomed to strangers occasionally walking through the front door, with money in hand, looking for something to buy: "This is some kind of store, ain't it?" But there were things that we kids never accepted.

Dad had his secrets about Oak Ridge; we kids had our own about how we hated the store building. As the year went along, we hoped that our folks were wondering why we never once brought any friends from church or school by this place. But they never asked.

We missed having a regular house, even the home

on Herbert Street. To top it all off, Grandpa Cagle came to Oak Ridge to work as a carpenter; and he moved in with us. At first, all of us, except Dad, wanted to return to Murphysboro.

Forty years later, I am asking myself: How was Mom able to manage a home in that building? I can't remember where she washed (but our clothes were clean and pressed), or how she cooked (but we ate as well as food rationing allowed). Guess I'll drive back down Central and look for the church—must have missed it on the way out.

Within a few minutes, I again park the car and get out to walk to a small graystone church.

In 1943, the Reverend Schultz had welcomed us like the displaced people we were—sort of. There were other families whose fathers were working at Oak Ridge but—so far as we knew—none living in a store building. But, no matter. We soon fell in ranks with a young people's group—about a dozen teenagers—that met every Sunday in church before catching a bus or streetcar to a real home for a social evening. We developed a certain group joy, a delight in each other, and we carried it wherever we went.

I am standing before the church door, remembering those young people so tangibly that I almost anticipate they will push through the door, right now, singing that old nonsense song that we used to sing:
> 'Twas midnight on the ocean,
> Not a streetcar was in sight.
> I stepped into the drugstore,
> to get myself a light . . .
> *(How does the rest of it go?)*

125

Adults, encountering us on the street, would shake their heads in gentle disapproval and smile, and go on with their serious business—just as I am doing now in returning to my car to drive to the hotel and check in. I have a conference to run.

Two days later, the national conference is proceeding as expected, with the giving of carefully structured papers that offend no one, followed by intense discussions forgotten after the first cocktail of the evening. We are now in recess so that the conferees may tour the World's Fair grounds at the university.

I opt instead to search for the old high school and, although aggravated by the changed landscape, I finally spot an imposing Jeffersonian-style building that must be Central High School.

In 1943, when we three scared kids from Murphysboro first approached it, my fears surrendered to admiration, because Central High—set prominently on a hilltop outside Knoxville—looked like a place of learning and of discipline. That's what it proved to be: excellent teachers, no talking or running in the halls, no swearing, no smoking, praise for good students, scorn and dismissal for the dull and the unruly. Katie Gresham's preparatory school for young ladies and gentlemen.

I park the car and walk toward the classic dome, carrying a briefcase in order to look official. Right off, I am disappointed by a sign that identifies this now as a junior high school (no mention of Central High).

But inside, it is still the same. There was Miss Ahler's Latin class, and Mr. Seymour's algebra; there, the English class where I sat by the girl with brown eyes and shiny bangs . . . oh my! The girl with shiny bangs.

126

She was the smartest girl in the class and she paid
attention to me only after I had memorized hundreds of lines of *Julius Caesar* and was paraded
before the class as an example of scholarship. I had
noticed her right away and had been startled by her
brown eyes and shiny brown hair, cut in bangs. On
the bus ride home from school, I found myself able
to recall her entire recitation, the soft but clear way
she spoke.

Then, we sort of began to walk together to the
bus stop. Shortly after the school year ended, I
awoke one morning, so possessed with images of
her that I telephoned from the pay phone next door
in the barbershop and arranged my first date.

There were other dates with her: talking through
ball games, holding hands in movies, walking by
the river.

The last time I talked with her was on the telephone. "Betty Ruth," I croaked mournfully, "you'll
not guess what has happened. We're movin'back to
Illinois! We're leavin' really soon. My dad has to go
to work down in Arkansas!"

She said that she would miss me, but that I could
surely come and visit—wouldn't I? And I replied
that, of course, I would come back—thinking that it
would never happen. Finally, there was nothing else
to say and I just hung up and never said another
word to anyone about the hole in my heart. (For
years afterward, I was mad at my sister, Agnes, for
insisting that we move back to Murphysboro so she
could spend her senior year at "Murphy High"; if
we had to leave Tennessee, at least I could have been
with Dad in Arkansas.)

The conference has adjourned amid a hail of
paper and absurd statements. It is midnight, and I
am awake in a penthouse suite (chairman's privi-

lege) that could accommodate a large family. The plush bar has gone unused; the parlor is undisturbed; the door to the view terrace is still locked — for, it is not Knoxville of the present that interests me. It is the past that is disturbing my sleep.

I get up and pull out the telephone directory and search for the family name of Betty Ruth: Hiscock. Nothing there. Moved? Dead?

I look out on the lights of Knoxville and remember the rest of the words of that nonsense song we used to sing:

> The man behind the counter
> was a lady old and gray,
> who used to peddle shoestrings
> on the road to Mandalay.
> Oh ain't we crazy!
> Oh ain't we crazy!
> That why the people call us nuts!
> Nuts!

The president of the Class of 1947 finally catches up with me in Omaha, explaining that I have been impossible to locate in time for the class reunion ("No one has moved so much") and relating details of the great time had by all. After running on for awhile, Ashman apologizes, "Well, let me give you a chance to ask about people . . . who haven't I

talked about?" I respond, "What about some of the teachers, Bob . . . what about Dozier?" Ashman hesitates, "Oh, he's been dead for years, Ed. Can you imagine anything ever killing Stephen B.!"

The Toughest Teacher

Agnes and Charley were just ahead of me in school, so I could profit from their experiences: find out the tough teachers and how you could cope with them. When they preceded me into Murphy High, one teacher's name kept coming up uncomfortably in our late afternoon sessions held in Mom's kitchen over sugar donuts and milk: "Dozier . . . Mr. Dozier." Agnes would say, "Mom, guess what Dozier did today? He asked Claude Rains a question that no one in class had been able to answer. Claude said, 'I don't know either.' Boy! you should have seen what happened then. Mr. Dozier went berserk! He ran around the room yelling at Claude: 'You don't know *either*! You don't know . . . either. I daresay that none of you assembled here to learn to read, to speak, and to write English know an *either*.' Mom, he just went on and on until Claude was almost crying. It really scared me."

A piece of donut stuck in my throat (that could have been me; I could have said that . . . easily!). One day I happened to ask Charley if he was, or was not, "goin' hikin'" with me. Charley really bawled me out: "Don't ever pronounce words like that! Say 'hiking!' Pronounce the 'g.' Dozier will skin you alive for that."

"I wasn't sayin' that," I complained. Charley just looked at me sadly and shook his head, "Boy are you going to get it!"

So the image of Mr. Stephen B. Dozier, teacher

and ogre, grew story by story: his use of sarcasm and public humiliation, his piercing intellect, his intolerance with dullness, and his anger at laziness.

Agnes graduated and went to college; Dad went away to help build another war plant. More importantly, I was scheduled for Dozier's English class. On the first Monday of class, he lectured on the necessity of exact expression and demanded that we keep notes of his lectures. (I wouldn't dare not try to record every word that he uttered!)

By Wednesday, Mr. Dozier had learned our names and had begun to zero in on our respective imperfections in grammar. "Jake (addressing the biggest tackle on the football team), you state that you cannot 'figger out' the imagery employed by the author Wilbur Daniel Steele in "Footfalls" . . . 'figure' used as a verb? Have you just arrived in this country, Jake?" And he was off on a tirade.

I kept waiting for my turn to come . . . for Mr. Dozier to get the best of me. I worried, and I worked and worked. I read all the assignments several times; I learned to use the library; I read and reread my class notes, even when I was sick. "One of these days . . . it will happen!" But it never did.

The grade of eighty-nine that I received at the end of the term was the lowest mark among my courses but a high mark for any boy in Dozier's class. But, the grade didn't seem to matter that much—a new attitude for me. What did matter is that I felt differently about myself—more confident—and knew who was responsible.

———————

In the years just before his death, Dad and I had our best talks—on all kinds of matters. But I steered us away from politics. Although Dad had always tolerated—maybe even enjoyed—my being different, he would never have understood how I could have voted for a Republican for president.

First a farmer's depression and then the Great Depression had rendered Dad a lifelong Democrat and caused him to enthrone Franklin Delano Roosevelt as "the savior of the common man." When the president spoke on the radio, none of us kids was permitted to talk—or even cough. Dad would lean intently over the old Gruen, nodding his head in full agreement, while drawing personal strength from every statement of FDR's.

"You're damned right!" he would exclaim. "You're damned right."

Tears for a Savior

April 12, 1945, was a fine day in southern Illinois. Facing into a gentle breeze that was full of smells of new life, we reluctantly made our way to high school. Charley was all for taking the day off but still followed me into the stuffy building. Trapped like all the rest of us.

In Latin II, while I was looking out the window and watching the seeds of the silver maple rotate their way to the ground, the warning bells rang, unexpectedly calling a general assembly. We students fled from the classrooms and flooded into the auditorium, anticipating a cause for celebration and maybe even a holiday. Hurrying along beside me, Lora Jean speculated, "I'll bet the war is over in Europe. That's got to be it!"

But when the principal continued to stand before us, unsmiling and grim, we knew it was something else.

"Attention, please . . . President Roosevelt has died," he announced. "All classes are suspended until day after tomorrow. I am sending you home to mourn . . . God bless this country."

Heading home, we complained about how the day had been ruined. None of us could remember any president besides FDR. To us, all previous presidents were more or less fictional characters. But not Roosevelt. His was the voice that calmed the nation through the fireside chats on radio: "My fellow Americans, I am absolutely confident that we will prevail . . . " His humor caused even my dad to laugh, as the president explained, "If my little dog Fella can understand the principle of lend-lease, why can't the opposition?"

Mom was in tears. I just took a spade from the shed and started turning over the garden. Bees were busy in the plum tree and little fluffy clouds floated by as I kicked the spade at the clay dirt. It was hard to imagine that someone that important in our lives could just up and die.

With every spadeful of earth, I began to conjecture that now the world would be different. Who would look out for poor people? Who would lead us through the rest of the war?

That evening, our neighbor, Hattie Boucher, ran over to get Mom. Dad was calling from the ordinance plant at Camden, Arkansas. When Mom returned she was wiping her eyes. "What'd Dad say, Mom?" we asked. "Wal . . . he wanted to talk about President

Roosevelt. He said it was like losing a father. Now, I'm going to tell you kids something you must never let on that I tole you: your Dad was cryin'."

David has eased the big boat from moorage and now we are cruising on Lake Kinkaid. My first time on the lake, but not the first time in this place. Other boats pass us—skiing and fishing parties. Not a one of them could begin to guess our mission.

Up Youngman's Branch, we cut the engine and glide over the site of the coal mine where, in 1935, Dad found the Christmas fox. David revs the engine and we quickly cross the lake and start looking for landmarks on rocky bluffs we once climbed. Triangulating our position with the bluffs, we back the boat off about a half-mile and switch on the depth sounder. We traverse back and forth, surveying the submerged terrain. Then we realize that we have found it: about sixty feet down there is a flat area, a few acres in size. That must be old "Lavinnie" Hutt's place.

We cut the engines and talk about her for awhile— and, too, about the boys who visited her long ago.

The Bird Woman

Charley, Ashman, and I hitched a ride west from Murphysboro with a rural mail carrier, who gave us some advice when he dropped us at Indian Creek

Bottoms: "Hikin' into the Kinkaid Hills, you say . . . well, you boys take care. It's dog days now and the copperheads will strike at anything. Watch where you put your butts and don't drink too much branch water."

We thanked him and took off through the woods to David's house, seeing nothing more threatening on the way than a thirsty terrapin looking for water.

David's mom, Aunt Lillian, gave us a send-off that made us feel like we were pioneers headed west to the Rocky Mountains. She packed four lunches of ham sandwiches and cookies and cautioned David to follow the lead of his older cousins—"Whatever happens."

And we did head west but only down the dusty old road past Grandpa's abandoned place (moved to town) and the shack on the hill, hidden now by the brush that had grown since we had lived there. As we hiked, we stirred up a cloud of brown road dust that traveled along with us. To the squirrels chatter-ing in the roadside oaks, we must have looked like a giant foraging centipede.

A couple of hours, and one small adventure later, we arrived at the base of dun-colored cliffs on the flanks of the Kinkaid Hills. In hiking cross-country toward the cliffs, we had kicked up a "spreadnad-der" and had come within an instant of killing the snake; but Miss Smith's biology lesson had taken hold, and we had let the harmless puff adder slither away. Concerned about rattlers, we now picked our way carefully up the gentlest incline we could find and flopped down on top of the bluff.

The ham sandwiches and the view revived us. We could see a couple of barn roofs, some gardens and hay fields, but mostly just treetops. Yep, as people moved to town, Kinkaid Valley was going back to wilderness.

"I could stay up here forever," Ashman said. "It's so peaceful."

"I'm dying of thirst," Charley admitted. He got no argument when he suggested that we head down to see if we could find a spring at the base of the cliffs, or some well water.

Working our way along the base of the cliffs, we broke through brush to find a bearded, half-naked man digging with a shovel. When he saw us, he swore loudly and scrambled away as if to grab something important. Each one of us must have thought "gun," for, we fled simultaneously—downhill, but in the same general direction. A little while later, Charley and I made contact on a dirt road. We yelled until we had gathered up Ashman and David.

"What do you suppose all that was about?" Ashman asked.

"I dunno. Maybe that guy has found the 'lost lead mine.'"

"I'd swear he was reachin' for a shotgun!"

"Wasn't he a wild-lookin' one!"

By now, we were parched and wobbly and were talking seriously about drinking out of a creek when we came upon a house (more of a shack), with a garden alongside and—"praises be!"—the unmistakable frame of a windlass well. Ashman was all for heading straight to a tin bucket hanging tantalizingly from a draw chain, but Charley and I said, "We've got to knock on the door and see if anyone is home."

As we walked toward the house, a very old woman stepped out and marched toward us. About ten feet away she stopped and looked us over. We did the best we could to keep from staring back at her bare feet, waist-length gray hair, very wrinkled face, and dress that looked like a tattered choir robe. We started to ask for water, but she cut off our words.

"Are you running to a war or away from one? . . . Hmm? I know one thing: you have scared away my birdies with all your yelling. The last time we had that much noise in the valley, the Illinois Central was running a train through here . . . yes! Where the Mudline Road now runs. Now, you boys draw yourselves a drink before you dry up and blow away."

"Yes, ma'am. Yes, ma'am! Thank you very much." The water was sweet and cold. The old woman came over and seemed to appreciate our relieved condition.

"You are welcome to sit down and rest awhile, but you must be very quiet and still while I feed my birdies." Fascinated, and with another round of "thank-yous," we sat down in the shade to watch. Pleased, she smiled (she still had teeth!), went into the house, and returned wearing a canvas apron having a row of pockets filled to overflowing with seeds and bread crumbs. Standing before us in a patch of sunlight, the old woman began to whistle in a high pitch, almost a hiss. Up from the garden flew a cardinal to land on her shoulder. The cardinal dropped down on the apron and began to feed in a pocket and kick food on the ground. That seemed to trigger the flight of dozens and dozens of wild birds to her. Flowing like a river of mixed species and colors they splashed over her—in hues of red, blue, yellow, and brown—prettying her hair and decorating her dress for an instant, fluttering around her apron, then settling on the ground to feed. Fascinated by this scene, at first we missed what she was rambling about:

These are my only friends . . . my loverly birdies . . . he left me long ago . . . took my Daddy's California money . . . I taught school

136

at Twin-Church School . . . he talked me into quitting . . . the passenger pigeons still came . . . I taught a lot of people who became somebody, merchants and attorneys . . . Daddy sent me to the dance in a pink satin gown . . . all the men wanted my hand . . . when the war with Cuba was over . . . we danced all night . . .

Coming back to the present, she fixed her eyes on us (I shivered): "What war will you boys fight? After the Germans are whipped, will it be the Russians? Money and killing . . . money and killing . . . and they will kill this valley someday. Oh, yes! The surveyors are already up here looking for a place to put a dam . . . But I shall not be . . . Oh! Who will feed my birdies?" She lowered her head and I thought she was crying. We were hushed.

Then, pointing toward the dirt road that led down to the Mudline, the old woman sent us solemnly on our way home. "You must leave now, but please get up very slowly . . . you are good boys. In town, you may tell them that you saw crazy old Lavinia Hutt feed her birdies."

The young woman whose hand I am holding has many admirable qualities: intelligence, wit, humor, even beauty . . . none of these attributes, nor all the wonders of medicine, will erase the fact that she is dying—nor postpone it much longer.

I sit and talk with Kristen when I can; she is good company. I tell her that yesterday, in the Coast Range, I heard a canyon wren and saw a crazy prairie falcon—that had no business being up in the mountains. She laughs and tells me again about the rare blue duck that she sighted on the Milford Track in New Zealand, during her last big trip.

We break conversation while the nurse services the medical paraphernalia attached to her. When we resume, Kristen confides: "I had a visitor yesterday who said, 'I know how you feel.' Ed, I was really rude to him. I said, 'You can't possibly know how it feels to be lying here dying at the age of twenty-seven!'" She was crying.

I touch her face and say, "Good for you, Kris! Yes. No one but you really knows."

The Shadow on the Window Shade

When I turned into our alley, I heard the fight between a man and a woman—their voices raised in rage. I was shocked to see our next door neighbors, the old grandma and grandpa, standing in their backyard—giving each other the devil. He was shoving his cane at her, more to keep her away—it appeared—than to do her any real harm. She was grabbing at his cane and yelling: "Lose your job, you lousy drunk! Go on and lose your job! Think you'll ever get another one? All you had to do was to sit on your ass at a junkyard. Can't even do that!"

The old man bellowed and swung his cane at her. Missing, he fell on the grass and lay there moaning. She looked at him in disgust and turned and went into the house.

I'd seen enough. I hurried into our house, where Mom was peeping out the kitchen window. "Oh Lordy, Edgar, old Mr. Swanson has been down at the tavern and gotten a snootful! His wife is sooo mad at him. He's supposed to be over at Wyde's Junkyard right now—on his night watchman job. Poor old man! And they need the money."

I agreed and got a glassful of milk. But I didn't feel sorry for the old couple; I felt sorry for the girl who lived with them—their granddaughter.

The Swanson house was so near ours that, at night, the shadows of its occupants appeared life-size on their window shades. Charley and I tried hard not to watch because the girl was not only beautiful, she was also very nice and talented. Some evenings when she was practicing the coronet, I would watch her shadow swaying to the music and wish that I were older. She never paid any attention to Charley or to me. The girl next door was too busy being smart, pretty, and perfect.

Yes, I really felt sorry for that girl and wished that I could do something to help her. If the old man lost his job . . . "Oh look," Mom exclaimed from the window. "Now, he's over at the well tryin' to draw up a bucket of water. If this wasn't so pitiful, I'd haf to laugh . . . oh! He about fell into that well!" Mom was laughing.

It came to me—what I had to do. "Mom," I asked painfully, "do you think it would be the right thing to do if I went over there and offered to walk him over to the junkyard? You know, he could lean on me. Once he got there, he wouldn't need to do anything but sleep in that big chair he always sits in. Mr. Wyde would drive by and see that he was on the job."

Mom viewed me with new respect. "Why Edgar . . . Edgar," she stammered, "I think that would be a wonderful thing to do." She added, "Love thy neighbor as thyself. That's what the Bible says!"

Mom was getting into it now, as I was heading for the door. She was telling me how to handle a drunk. "First thing you do is offer to draw him a drink of water. He'll see you're friendly and the water'll help to sober him up."

It worked. Old Mr. Swanson lowered the cane and watched me pulling the chain. He put the cup of water to his lips, pulled it away looking disappointed, but went ahead and drank most of it. "Mr. Swanson," I said, "what do you say we walk over to your job. No one will yell at you over there. You can lean on me."

He mumbled something and grinned, and about knocked me down when he took my arm. Stumbling and lurching, arms around each other, we dodged our way out to the street, where he started singing a little song. We hadn't gone far when I began to see faces peering out windows and people coming out on their front porches to watch our weaving, halting progress along three blocks of Herbert Street. I heard some laughter, and some kids stopped a game of streetball and jeered at us. I didn't care—except that I hoped that the girl had seen us leave, had noticed my good deed.

Handling a drunk was a lot harder than I had imagined. I was glad to deposit old Mr. Swanson in his guard chair and hurry back home. Maybe Mrs. Swanson and the girl would come out and say something to me.

Their yard was vacant when I walked slowly across it, and not a sound came from their house. Well, I could always see her at school.

At supper, Mom told me that Mrs. Swanson had watched us going down the street. "I'm sure she'll

140

be thankful," Mom said. "I've never seen him that way—that bad. Maybe that will be the last of it."

And it was the last of it. Because when I "just happened" to run into the neighbor girl in the library—after she had been avoiding me at every opportunity, she snatched up her books and stood up from the table where I had joined her. Glaring at me she whispered, "You stay away from me! Don't you ever come near my family again! You have made us a laughing stock!"

It was a long time before I even raised my eyes from my textbook. I took the long way home so I could avoid walking by the Swanson house.

Off the coast of Norway, a feeling comes from long ago. Maybe it is the peaceful look of the little villages tucked away on shore; perhaps it is the smell of their hay fields. But it is as real as it is subtle.

For a moment I am young again . . . in the spring . . . at twilight . . . headed home for supper . . . smelling the first green grass of the year, seeing the first leaves . . . feeling the goodness of the time and the harmony of the world.

Miss Esther Smith

Hours later I was still jubilant. She had said it allright! Just as clear as a bell, "My, but you have a fine mind." When I walked into Mom's kitchen and

141

threw down my books, I was still reconstructing the event—the way Miss Smith had paused and looked me right in the eye, the certainty in her voice.

So I told Mom, who looked pleased, but offered some advice:

"Well, Edgar, you are smart, but don't count your chickens before they hatch. You're not out of high school yet."

I argued, "But Mom, I really thought this out. You see, I read Mendel's Law of Heredity, and the more I read it, the more I realized that it doesn't jive with the story of Adam and Eve in the Book of Genesis. We have too much genetic variety to have come from just two people."

"Well . . . no teacher should be criticizing the Bible, laws of Mendel or not!"

"Mom, Miss Smith didn't say anything about the Bible! I came up with that myself. She is just trying to teach us about the scientific method."

"All right son. But you have to remember that the Bible was written a long time ago and you just can't read it like some textbook. It's still the word of God."

"I know that, Mom . . . thanks for the donuts." And I was off to collect leaves of different species of deciduous trees.

Miss Smith did things like that—I mean causing people to think and to argue. You would never suspect it to look at her: small and kind of plain looking, except when she was talking about something important to her. Then she could really hold your attention.

For days after it happened, Ashman and I were still talking about Miss Smith's "sex lecture"—that's what it was called by the students. But the school jocks kept saying, "She's the last woman in the world who would know anything about sex . . . look at that flat chest!"

Those jocks must not have been listening. Wow! What incredible information she was dispensing. Ashman and I could recall, together, almost every word of the "sex lecture." That lecture stimulated many evening philosophical discussions between us—the profundity of discussion rising with the moon and the lateness of the hour. The main points of the lecture went something like this (with Miss Smith referring to large-sized illustrations mounted on an easel):

> This single cell organism, a female gamete, travels down the fallopian tube (here) and joins a male gamete to become a zygote. It attaches to the womb (here). Each of you once looked like this. From this stage you had only a few months to become an individual. Through mitosis, cell division, you rapidly become an embryo (here). At this stage the cells are becoming highly specialized, already differentiating to perform functions such as food assimilation and waste removal.
>
> Now, notice something very important! This is a photograph of a tadpole. Compare it to an early stage of the human embryo. See the similarities in structure (here and here)—especially the gills. Look also at some of these other stages of development of *Homo sapiens* as compared to other organisms. We see in this evidence of a very important principle: the human embryo passes through the stages of the more primitive (less-developed or less-specialized) forms of life, as it advances toward birth. The scientific phrase for this is: ontogeny recapitulates phylogeny.
>
> It is as if the creator of the universe, while performing a series of magical acts, makes a special announcement: "Now! for my greatest miracle, I give you . . . not a sponge, or a fish, or an amphibian . . . or even a monkey, but a human being."

Some of us students heard and saw a lot more of Miss Smith throughout the year, for she was especially generous in hauling us around in her old station wagon so we could observe the extraordinarily diverse flora and fauna of Little Egypt. But when I think of Miss Esther Smith at her best, I recall that dramatic lecture that—more than all the formal religious instruction that I had received—declared the glory of creation. I always intended to tell her that.

"She asked about you," Ashman said, telling me he found her sorting biological specimens for yet another year of students.

"Hair still short," he laughed, "and those awful field clothes," reminding me of the eccentric, superb teacher we loved.

"She's pleased you won honors. . . . Saw it in the paper," he added, and I imagined the sparkle in her eyes and the smile.

"I owe her," I observed, determining that I would write, when I became famous, or at least very wise.

My friend and professional colleague has died. He was always—first—a friend. Only two months ago we were planning that trip to Zamboanga (and it almost came off). He was to do the geology and I would do the hydrology of those coal mines that the Filipinos wanted to dewater. With gun ships hovering about to protect us from the Moros, it would indeed have been a last hurrah for two old guys like

us. Now, this God-awful funeral. "Preacher, you
do not speak of the Tom Friz that I knew." No, that
one is somewhere else now with the sun on his neck
and the horizon before his eyes.

Peggy

On a spring day I skipped track practice and
walked Barbara Thorp home from high school—
admiring her all the way but never telling her so. I
left her at the corner of the block and turned down
the alley toward home. Mom and some neighbors
were standing in the backyard staring at the
ground.

I entered the yard and saw that they were watching my dog Peggy: she was staggering and
slobbering around the backyard. I dropped my
books and ran toward her, but Mom caught my arm
and said, "Now Edgar! I don't believe there's anything we can do."

I answered sharply, "She was all right when I left
for school." I knelt by Peggy who had fallen on her
side and was wheezing as if she had something
caught in her throat. She seemed to be in agony, but
she wagged her tail a little. I patted her head and
said, "Good dog—good Peggy."

"Mom," I pleaded. "can't we get a doctor?"

"Honey, she's dying. She's been failin' for some
time—you've been too busy to notice."

I sat down and put Peggy's head on my lap and
began to pet her and thought about the years
before.

(I saw Peggy peeking through the green of the
woods. She was playing hide-and-seek with Charley
and me. "Good dog, Peggy!" we yelled. "Git that
snake!" More than likely, before the day was over,
Peggy would find a copperhead while she was out

145

scouting ahead of our bare feet. We would find her
with jaws locked behind that old snake's head just
whipping him to death. Peggy was our guardian
while we herded cows, picked berries, or were out
just running around.)

Charley came through the backyard, paused, and
went into the house without saying a word. I was
grateful. We all knew that Peggy was, mostly, my
dog. The neighbors had gone home and there was
only Mom, Peggy, and me. Peggy was wheezing
something awful now and blowing bubbles of
blood.

"Oh, Mom, what can we do! What can we do?"

"Sometimes, Son, you can't do a thing."

(Dad was singing his song about Peggy O'Neil
and the singing of her name was embarrassing
Peggy so that she was sneezing, barking, and running around us in a circle of dust. We were headed
down the road to Sunday dinner at Grandpa's.

Dad had a deep, powerful voice:

> Peggy O'Neil was a girlie was she.
> Aha! Aha! Aha!
> Sweet personality, grown-folk's suprisality.
> That was Peggy O'Neil.)

Mom came over and put her hand on my shoulder. "I think she's dead, Son. I'll get Grandpa to
bury her."

I laid Peggy's head down, gently on the grass, and
stood up. Somehow it had become almost night.
The houses on Herbert Street wore black shadows
and yellow jack-o'-lantern windows. Mom and I
stood for a while and listened to the families at supper. Then we went into the house.

Many of us who were teenagers in World War II were—during that time—a poorly fathered bunch, experiencing more symbolic fatherhood than intimate association. Our fathers just weren't around much from 1941 to 1946. They were away building war plants or fighting in the war. Oh, we received some letters, a few phone calls . . . and admonitions from our moms: "Now, you just wait until your father hears about this!" But, the bottom line was that we had to work out a lot of things—without our fathers.

The Boy Who Loved Wild Things

One day a woman came to our door and said to my mom: "I understand that your son is very good in algebra. Would he be willing to tutor my son? I will pay two dollars an hour." Mom accepted the job for me.

Pleased and nervous, I walked to the woman's home, doing a double take when I arrived because a gold star hung in the window to announce that someone in that household had died in the war. When she admitted me to the house, the woman explained that the star was for her husband, who had been killed in Sicily.

Then I was introduced to my pupil, her son, Montgomery. He had a terrible scowl that did not fade when we sat at the dining table to begin the first lesson. Realizing that my tutoring adventure was about to end before it could even start, I tried to draw him out by telling him a little about myself. When I mentioned the hill country, it seemed that he became a different person. "Oh," he said. "that's where I go to collect." After he told me about his field trips, we were able to study algebra, and we also began to share a deep interest in wild things and the outdoors that continued for the remainder of my time in high school.

The algebra lessons soon fell into a pleasant routine. For about two hours, Montgomery and I would grind through the equations. Then, I would begin to comment—somewhat loudly—that he had mastered the week's assignments. In the adjoining living room, his mother would clear her throat and speak to us: "Now, you're sure that he has it down, Edgar? He *is* doing better in the exams. All right, you can go downstairs."

Whereupon Montgomery's face would light up, and we would head for the basement steps. I always let him go first—just in case. One whole wall of the basement was lined with glass cages mounted on a wooden deck. Neon lights cast an eerie spell over the scene as we started at one end and went down the line, lifting cage lids and saying hello to old friends and to new arrivals. Here a Massaauga rattlesnake, fat and smartly dressed in diamond patterns of brown and ivory; next a five-foot-long, black-and-yellow-bellied king snake curling around Montgomery's arm. "I let them go every spring," Montgomery told me. "It's not fair to cage wild things—for very long."

After we had viewed all his friends—snakes, lizards, and salamanders—we would return upstairs for the ritualistic end of our session. His mom would exclaim, "Oh, Edgar, you should hear how well Montgomery is progressing on the violin!" Montgomery would then frown, pick up the violin (his father's), and scratch out some awful sounds while I tried to look appreciative.

By the time Montgomery had passed algebra, he and I and another youth, whose father was away, were sharing field trips—sometimes collecting, but mostly just observing and wondering together about the physical world we were fast discovering. I recall the spring day when we saw our first Prothonotary warbler—an abundance of gold flitting through a sassafras grove. Sometimes during the peak of the spring bird migration, we would sit together in the thickets in Indian Creek Bottoms, watching wave after wave of warbler and sparrow moving through the understory all around us. We took field notes and marveled at the varieties of color, shape, and song—celebrating when we experienced our first sighting of a species that we identified using Peterson's field manual. I remember that Montgomery could not stay away from snakes. On one of our trips he captured a large copperhead. Although he secured it in a canvas bag, we made him walk apart, far to the rear.

In terms of the high school society, we amateur naturalists must have appeared as an odd lot, respected—as I remember—by the biology teacher but liked by few students. We certainly didn't raise the level of competition for best athlete, most popular student, or king of the prom.

I went away, eventually becoming a scientist. The others also became scientists—Montgomery, a professor of biology.

Then, one day—years later—Montgomery killed himself.

I am told that, just as summer was fading into fall and another school year was upon him, he walked way out into the country along an old railroad track, and there he shot himself. I know the look and feel of that country, during that season. There would have been little green and orange grasshoppers shying away from his path. It would have been like him to muse that they, vulnerable to the first hard frost, would still outlive him.

There would probably have been a wind off the big lake. Perhaps he noticed that the tiny purple asters were about their fall business of providing spore for the wind. The evening primrose are particularly beautiful at that time of year. Maybe he noticed one last time how they gather the gold of the setting sun.

Somewhere in Hawaii, amid flowers and rainbows, I realize that I have never written about my Grandma Imhoff—Arah, the quiet one. I have passed over her—I suppose—because unlike my other grandparents, she never told her own story. I mean, she never told it in words.

Images of Arah

My first memory of Grandma Imhoff is of this distant view of a lone figure coming more and more into focus as we kids scuffle along on our way home from Mt. Joy School. It is an image of an old woman in a long dress standing in the corner of a yard we intend to cross. She stands motionless looking down the path toward us.

As we approach, we see that, of course, it is Grandma. Who else would be wearing an old gingham bonnet—even in this heat? Who else would look at us in quite this way through horn-rimmed glasses and smile and say, "I have sugar cookies in the oven." We take her flour-dusted hands and clutch at her apron, and she leads us into her kitchen as if we were the finest, most precious children in all the world.

At an early age, we kids had heard enough gossip to know that Grandpa Imhoff "bossed" Grandma. Mom told Dad, "You'll never boss me like that, Ernie Imhoff!" But I once heard someone use the word *overshadowing* and that seemed to be more like it.

Grandpa was a man who stood out in a crowd, the old folks would recall during the gossiping sessions that the Mt. Joy Church members called "reunions" and "socials." I would hang around the crochet circles and chairs of whittlers—a small, big-eared boy gathering tidbits of the family. I learned that Grandpa Imhoff was considered quite a catch— "until he inherited next to nothin"—who "could put a bushel of wheat on each shoulder and walk it straight up a ladder."

All I ever heard about Grandma was that she had been a Heiple and that the Imhoffs and the Heiples had come here together from Pennsylvania. The old folks reasoned that Arah Heiple was bound to marry Charley Imhoff, "cause they went together a long time."

When I was a teenager, my Aunt Hazel was showing me some old photographs. I was taken with the image of a pretty girl with long wavy hair. "Who was she?" I asked. "Why, that's your Grandmother Arah when she was a bride. She had the most beautiful auburn hair and gray eyes."

I was flabbergasted. I could not visualize that girl in the photograph as becoming the grandma who had baked the sugar cookies. My grandma's hair was gray and always tied into a bun. Grandma's face was nice—but old.

That day I resolved I would ask Grandma Imhoff about her childhood, and about her and Grandpa when they were young. I wanted especially to probe a little into the nature of their relationship: had they ever been in love? I had seen Grandpa being stingy with her and I had heard him scold her about planting so many flowers—which she did—all along the house, the garden, and by the well. "Arah! This winter we won't be able to eat them flowers." Grandma would just smile and go about her own business in a soft, steady way.

I could understand and forgive Grandpa's stinginess; he had the poorest land in the county. Still, I wondered about the things he said to her like, "Arah! Why are you a standin' there looking at the sky, we got milkin' to do!"

Grandma Arah never told me how she felt about such things. When she was on her deathbed, however, I found out about them. I looked in and saw him holding her . . . saw their faces . . . and I found out about them.

———————————

I have been associating with politicians so long that I can think like them: scary admission—that. The public has only seen the tip of the iceberg. Many of us career federal executives fantasize about "telling it all" . . . someday. But, I doubt if we ever will, because we have become too much a part of the political system.

Politics involves the art of symbolism and the practice of deceit. Heck! I remember the time you could learn that on a vacant lot in Murphysboro— for just a dollar. Today, it's the same show, same tricks; just costs you a lot more.

The Medicine Show

We felt half-ashamed being there: high school students should know better than to attend an old-fashioned medicine show. "Such quackery!" But Mr. Wathan, our history teacher, had said, "You boys ought to see at least one medicine show. After the war, they will disappear from the American scene." So, there we were, Charley and I, standing with the rest of the yokels gathered around a stage and tent—waiting to be entertained, if not cured.

Three banjo players appeared in blackface costumes and makeup—tattered clothing, huge red lips, and white eyes. In between numbers, they jokingly humiliated each other about being lazy, lovesick, and afraid.

After the banjo players exited to a roaring applause, a tall Negro man limped on stage, hunched over and moving as in agony. "Hey,

Clarence!" said the master of ceremonies, "what fo'
you crawl aroun' lak dat?" Then Clarence and the
MC began to discuss Clarence's many ailments.
After a description of each problem (usually with
references to sex, sleep, or bowels), the MC would
offer Clarence a drink from a flat green bottle he
pulled from his coat pocket. At first Clarence would
reluctantly accept a small swig, but as he found his
ailments miraculously disappearing, he would drink
deeper and deeper and stand taller and taller. After
polishing off two bottles, Clarence was jumping
around the platform, laughing and praising "Whatever you got in dat little bottle. Sho has done me
good! Sho has! I'd better go tell the missus. She
gawn be s'prised . . . oops! (holding his straw hat
over the fly on his trousers) . . . as well as dee-
lighted! Uh uh!" And Clarence exited and the crowd
was hollering and howling with laughter.

The MC slapped his sides and laughed and
laughed with the crowd. Then he licked his lips and
raised his hands to bring silence.

> 'Folks,' he said, 'we've had a little fun here
> tonight, but that is not why we have come to
> the fair city of Murphysboro. No. We have
> come to bring you a medicine so powerful that
> Dr. Livingstone himself, that great and coura-
> geous man who discovered this magic life
> tonic, hesitated his whole life in revealing the
> secret. Two years ago, my associates and I dis-
> covered the lost secret that Dr. Livingstone
> brought out of Africa—the secret my friends of
> the chemical ingredients of the tonic used by
> members of the Kooyamongo tribe to prolong
> life to a hundred and fifty years and potency to
> a hundred years! Now we believe that it is
> God's mission for us to make this available to
> every American who will listen to our story,

and—as God is our witness—that is what we shall do.

Yes, Clarence was just acting up, here on this stage tonight. No medicine, however powerful, can act that fast on that many ailments. But, as God is my witness, I tell you that my friend Clarence was indeed in just that kind of condition when he came to our tent in Memphis not six months ago. After very few treatments (one bottle per treatment) he was a totally changed man.

Friends, . . . I bring to you a gift so precious that it would be evil . . . evil . . . I say, to profit from bestowing this upon you. No more bent back! No more weak lungs! No more cramping bowels! Goodbye, cancer . . . goodbye, you devil!

My associates are going to pass through the crowd with bottles of Dr. Livingstone's Life Tonic. Now, don't shove and grab. We'll stay here until everyone gets a chance to receive this precious medicine. Just one dollar a bottle, folks! That's our cost in bringing this gift to you. Raise your dollars high.

I turned to Charley and whispered, "Boy is he going to be surprised. No one will buy this stuff."

On the contrary, the medicine man knew his crowd. Green dollars sprouted from the crowd like corn after the first rain. The medicine men worked quickly through the field of waving arms, plucking the dollars with one hand while shoving bottles with the other. As they toiled the MC continued to sing the praises of Dr. Livingstone's Life Tonic.

_____

They are waiting with lights on and pie hot and are upon me gently when I step out of the car. "Edgar, we'd about given up on you," Mom says, as I hug her. Dad looks smaller. "Well, well . . ." he says, gripping my hand. "It's been a long time."

The coconut cream pie stands five inches high at the center. I need it like a job in Washington, D.C., but I do need the news of the tribe. "____is divorced and living in an apartment. Her boss is making passes at her. ____is out of work in the mines and his diabetes is killing him. Your uncle, poor thing, can't remember a thing—has Altzheimer's disease (I am indeed sorry!). ____has mortgaged his home to pay for ____'s baby (it figures). Your Grandma Cagle knows you're a comin' and wants to see you (okay)."

We recite into the night the litany of the family—the dead and the living, the near and the distant. It is an old, carefully structured exercise to allow me to belong . . . to permit me, the wandering sheep, to rejoin the flock. Finally, Mom poops out and goes to bed. I follow Dad out to the porch where we sit while he smokes and coughs. The cicadas are singing the summer song of the South. Dad asks, "Son, do you remember that time we went down and saw all them snakes? Wasn't that something!"

The Snake Dens

The fat and determined six-foot rattler finally did it: unnerved Dad. Until then, Dad had been a good sport about the snake dens—playing the role of a father home from the war plants, eager to catch up on the activities of his sons. I was studying biology, huh. Well, he would be glad to take a field trip with me. "Just south of Cobden, was it? At the base of the rocky bluffs by the Big Muddy River?" He was game. We would drive down there and take a nice hike.

And he had been game. (Anyone who can qualify for five engineering licenses through night study at a kitchen table has to have guts.) The situation, however, was that he was being weakened by attrition. The rattler blocking our path was the twenty-second snake that we had seen so far on this spring day—in one mile of hiking. Its head, big as a man's fist, moved menacingly toward us as if to measure the intruder. Then the head would snap back into the coil, ready to strike.

Frankly, it was beginning to unnerve me. This rattler was not following the behavior pattern that my biology teacher, Miss Smith, had described when she had shown the class this trail last winter: "If you leave them alone, they will just crawl away. The species *Crotalus adamenteus* is really a gentle species."

Dad was beginning to say "sonofabitch" over and over. When I was younger, that meant run. But where to now? We had just passed a big cottonmouth draped in a low tree (yes, they will do that, near water). Not fifty feet back we had shooed a copperhead off the trail. Our whole back trail was strewn with snakes coming out and up for their first sunbath of the year—and their first snack. The day had warmed since we had started this tentative hike

157

two hours ago. There would be more snakes back there now. The shorter part of the trail lay ahead.

Behind me, Dad's speech was showing the results of his years of association with construction tradesmen as he moved along to far more colorful phrases. I could sense him beginning to do something desperate, but I didn't want to take my eyes off the rattler that would not budge from our path (Miss Smith would say, "its habitat").

"Dad? Whatcha doin'?"

"I'm gettin' me a big stick to kill that ____ ____. That's what I'm doing!"

"Dad . . . be careful. You don't want to scare up somethin' else."

Caar-rack! Dad was armed. I didn't have time to look back, because at the sound of the breaking branch the snake struck at me—coming up about two feet short. When he did that, the old snake lost the friendship and understanding of an amateur biologist. I joined Dad as primitive man.

Whack. Whack. Whack. Dad was flailing away.

"He's still moving, Dad! Give me that club!"

Together we stepped over the remains of a splendid specimen of C. adamanteus and worked our way back to the car. No need to tell Miss Smith about this field trip.

By the time they located me, it was too late to go to Cousin David's funeral. Now, I am sitting here, trying to write a letter to his family, but still not accepting his unexpected death.

What shall I say? Not: "I regret that we, who were once so close, spent so many years apart." Not: "I just wish we had one more day together. We would drive out to the old place and look around . . . maybe find the foundations of the house . . . the creek." No, for about now David would be losing patience: "Aw, Ed! For Chrissakes!" He would scold me. "Write 'em a nice letter and get on with your life."

Cousin David was like that. Suddenly, I miss him very much.

Crossing the Field

Mom reminded me that I would be leaving in a few months. "It's such a nice spring day," she suggested. "Why don't you hitch a ride out to the country to see David one last time at their place? They'll be movin' into town soon. I'll run next door and phone them you're comin'."

"That's a good idea, Mom. I've been runnin' five miles a day anyway. I can be out there in no time."

And I was, running along the highway, through the woods, and then up the hill to the Evans' house. Aunt Lillian and Cousin David came out, grinning and happy to see me.

"I'm sure glad you could come," Lillian said. "Lord knows when we'll see you again."

"Oh, I'll be back," I assured her.

"It seems like only yesterday you and David were little boys. Remember how you and Charley used to come over and stay over night, and we used to have the darndest time tryin' to git youin's to go to sleep. 'Giggle, giggle; jabber, jabber' . . . seems like jist yesterday. Now Charley's overseas in the Army and you're leavin' to go to college." Aunt Lillian wiped her eyes with her apron.

"Aw, Mom! For Chrissakes!" David scolded. "We're going to go out and look around the place."

I looked back and waved when Aunt Lillian called after us, "I'm fixin' ham salad and apple pie for dinner. You boys be back here in 'bout an hour."

"I don't know why she always does that," David said. "She's always worrying about my goin' away to college. I told her not to fuss, because I'm not going."

We walked down in the pasture to where the old horse, Jude, had been struck by lightning. Only the bleached thigh bones were left. "That was the stubbordest animal Dad ever had," David declared.

We walked up the creek a ways to where Charley, David, and I had dammed it during a heavy rain. We had pushed in hay bales, limbs, and rocks until a pool of water formed up to our armpits. When it washed out, we were flushed halfway down the hill. "Remember how mad your mom was when we came in all covered with mud and half-drowned?" David laughed.

How can you be sure you're not goin' to college?" I asked David.

He halted under a big oak tree that still had an iron hitching ring embedded in its trunk. We sat down in the shade and looked over toward Grandpa's place and to the Kinkaid Hills beyond.

"I don't know," David answered. "I'm just not cut out for it, I guess."

"Hey, you're smart, David. As smart as any of us," I argued.

"Maybe. But I can't see leavin' this part of the country. This is all I want—Mt. Joy, this land, Murphysboro . . . maybe I'm not like you, Edgar!"

I let it be. The hawks were hunting over the fields where I had helped David set his fox traps, piling up small mounds of manure and baiting the traps with chicken meat, before burying the traps in the mounds.

We walked back to the house, by way of the barn. "It's tumblin' down," David said, kicking the loose siding. "Dad just doesn't have time between the farm and his highway job."

As always, Aunt Lillian had made a marvelous meal. She looked at me mischievously. "Wal . . . are you goin' to git yourself a girlfriend in college, Edgar?" I was embarrassed.

"I probably won't have time for girls," I said. "That scholarship won't pay everything."

"Oh, you'll have time!" she said. Her eyes flashed and she laughed, looking years younger. "You'll have time."

We stood around the kitchen visiting with Aunt Lillian while we did the dishes. She told us, again, about the yard dances that people used to hold. "When there was life out here in the country . . . lots of young people at Mt. Joy."

Then we went out and sat in the yard one last time. Aunt Lillian asked me again if I was going to be a preacher.

"I don't know what I'm going to be," I said. "I'm just goin' to see what happens."

After I left them, I looked back once to see them still standing in the yard. They had watched me all the way across the field. I waved briefly and followed the trail into the woods.

Last night I had this vivid dream (a REM event, an analyst would say) in which I rub a bottle and attract a genie who is willing and able to answer any question I would care to ask. "But, just one question," she cautions. "Ask with care." Aware of this unusual opportunity, I contemplate for quite a while. Finally, pleased with the question I am about to ask—the answer to which will make me the wisest person in the world, I say: "What is time?" The genie looks impressed. "Time . . . ah, time," she says. "Time is . . . uh oh! (looking frantically at her wristwatch). Got to go now. I'm late." And she just begins to fade away. "Wait!" I yell. "You must answer!" I awake to the ticking of the alarm clock and to the moon shining through my bedroom window.

Peaches and Moonlight

During the days of dead summer, when the men were at World War II, the peaches of Little Egypt were picked by women, old men, and boys and girls who swarmed over the hilltop orchards doing the best they could to start the sequence of rushed events that, each nightfall, would send trainloads of the perishable commodity north for icing. Each night of the season, I would wait on an elevated platform in Murphysboro, with the rest of an icing crew composed of old men and boys, while boxcars and boxcars of peaches were pushed onto the siding by the ice plant. When the train stopped, we boys on the crew would leap on top of the boxcars ("recklessly," said the old men), open the lids of the refrigeration bunkers, and frantically fix a portable chute between the platform and the boxcars. Then, we would leap about from platform to car to platform, breaking ice and shoving blocks of it down the chutes to fill the bunkers that would "ice" the peaches. The old men would supply us with big cakes of ice and would curse and laugh to see us getting so little done with so much energy.

We took their remarks as good-natured kidding, for we would not have traded places with any of the boys now asleep in the quiet town. I could almost feel my muscles grow with each shove of a one-hundred-pound load. This was a man's work: to put fresh peaches on the table, soon, in St. Louis, Kansas City?—just about anywhere.

The night we iced the last trainload of the season, we worked under a full moon. It was an unusual night in other ways, too, because someone finally fell off a boxcar—busting an ankle—and later, the last boxcar derailed. While the railroad crew was retracking the car, we boys rested on the platform and listened to the old men talk about the places they had been and the things they had done.

By the time we iced the last of the peaches, it was the wee hours of the morning. As I began a lonely walk home, the moon was falling fast causing big shadows between houses and under the trees.

I knew there was just me out tonight, but gradually there arose the feeling that I might not be totally alone . . . somewhere there in the shadow of the Collins' house, a movement? . . . the faint sound of running feet and excited breath, the way we once played kick-the-can on this street . . . under the big maple tree, blotches of moonlight on the grass . . . looking so much like kids sitting in a circle . . . from the shadowy porch where the Lawler boy once played his sad trumpet, a gleam as of brass . . . impossible! . . . he was killed in the Pacific . . . silly . . . almost all the kids but me have left.

I entered the last shadow of our front porch and sat down softly in the swing so that it would not creak and scare Mom. Then I looked up and down the street for a while, trying to fix forever how I felt about these people and this place.

Epilogue

A Life among Strangers

Little remains of the pioneer community that formed around Mt. Joy Lutheran Church. The blacksmith shop and grade school disappeared long ago. All the giant oaks are gone. The church almost survived to become a registered historical building, but a tornado damaged it beyond the capacity of local donations. The last time I was there my grown daughter flew in from the East and joined me in a visit to the old cemetery—which we were pleased to find well maintained. Kat was enthralled with the many repetitions of our family name. Growing up all over this nation, she had become accustomed to us being the only Imhoffs in a community, or even a state. Kat made a game out of locating the tombstone of Wylie, Charles, Arah, and other names from the bedtime stories I had told to her and my son, Scott.

The Kinkaid Hills seemed smaller and nearer than I had remembered. We did not bother to hunt for the hill where the shack once stood. For Chuck and David had said they were over there once, looking around for relics (of the people who had lived there), and found only some broken dishes and a broken doll that must have belonged to Agnes.

A few years after that last visit to Mt. Joy, I made an emergency trip to Murphysboro. On the way down from St. Louis, I decided to detour—north of town—to see if I could find the Nolte Place. It was there, all right, but it is no longer a small farm out in the country. Development had taken our pasture, the orchard, and the weed field that Charley and I used for cover

165

when we would sneak away from hoeing and plowing. The road has been paved and is designated by fancy signs as a national bike trail. The old Number 5 School building, just down the road, appears to have been converted into a home. Surely those people are haunted by both laughter and tears.

Completing my arrival, I drove into Murphysboro, passing Tower Grove Cemetery where, I am told, Cousin David now lies. I drove so slowly along the brick streets of my hometown and gawked so much, that the natives—except for the Missouri tags—would have taken me for a realtor. Murphysboro still looks like a good place for growing up.

Sentiments welled up in me as I drove out these trails of my youth—where almost every building, street corner, and lot has a meaning and carries a memory. But one of those feelings was of alienation.

Grandma Cagle would have set me straight. She would have said: "Hon, what did you expect? . . . spendin' your life among strangers!"

Edgar Allen ("Ed") Imhoff has recently retired from a long career in geosciences and management and lives in Davis, California. Ed has worked throughout the United States, holding responsible positions in private industry, academe, and government. His professional honors include The William C. Ackermann Award for Excellence in Water Management and the title of Meritorious Senior Executive conferred by the president.

Ed's professional writings have appeared in publications of the U.S. Geological Survey, the American Association for the Advancement of Science, and various similar organizations. Although he has long dabbled in creative writing, *Always of Home: A Southern Illinois Childhood* is his first major nontechnical work.